VOICES *of*
RAWMARSH
& PARKGATE

VOICES *of*
RAWMARSH
& PARKGATE

ANTHONY DODSWORTH

The
History
Press

Frontispiece: Betty and Lavinia Wright in the Whit Parade on Rawmarsh Hill.

First published 2009

The History Press Ltd
The Mill, Brimscombe Port
Stroud, Gloucestershire, GL5 2QG
www.thehistorypress.co.uk

Reprinted 2011

British Library Cataloguing in Publication Data.
A catalogue record for this book is available from the British Library.

ISBN 978 0 7524 4842 8

Typesetting and origination by The History Press Ltd.
Printed in Great Britain

CONTENTS

Fun and games in a snowy playground at Netherfield Lane School in the 1950s.

ACKNOWLEDGEMENTS

Many people have helped in the completion of this project by providing memories, photographs and information; I am very grateful to them all, especially those who showed such patience in answering all my questions. I would particularly like to thank the following:

Harold Badger, Elsie Beaumont, Harry Beaumont, Cyril and Joyce Bray, Malcolm and Noreen Brown, Margaret Chambers, Les Coe, Mollie Cooper, Albert Evans, Jim Evans, Leslie Evans, Reg and Mary Ferns, Ted Frost, Joan Gillions, Ray Hague, George Hallam, Yvonne Harrison, Cliff and Joyce Hawley, Ray Hearne, Frank and Margaret Horner, Mary Hutchinson, Danny Larder, Ron Liversidge, Evelyn Longden, Henry Lowry, Marian Overland, Marjorie Oxer, Stephen Oxer, Joan Pearce, Edna Pease, Gordon Read, June Roberts, Edith Schofield, Nellie Schofield, Chris Sharp ('Old Barnsley', Barnsley Market), Sheila Skeldon, Freda Stacey, the staff of Rotherham Archives and Local Studies Library, Len and Muriel Sykes, David Sykes, Dorothy Taylor, Anne Thompson, Elizabeth Totterdell, John and Betty Turner, Edna Vaughan, Bryan and Helena Ward, Betty Watts, Anne Whitehouse and Betty Wright. Many thanks also to Jane, my wife, who has done so much to help me with this project. I apologise if I have omitted the name of any contributor.

I would also like to record my thanks to the following students at St Pius X Catholic High School, Wath-upon-Dearne, for helping me with some of the interviews: Jack Prendergast, Bridey Seekings, Aiden Stone and Joe Ward.

INTRODUCTION

When anyone takes up family history nowadays they are always encouraged by expert guides to begin by talking to surviving older members of their family. For enthusiasts of local history the need to talk to older people long resident in a locality is often not stressed in initial guidelines, even though the memories of such people can provide a rich and varied source of information. In the past, many people thought that historical information could only be accessed through painstaking study of old books and documents in archives and libraries. Today we are tempted to think that a thorough knowledge of how to use Google and the internet will provide us with all we need to know about a locality's past. In truth a deep understanding of the historical development of a place today is only likely to be achieved by using a wide range of different sources. One of the key sources should be the oral memories of older people who have lived through the changes in their community over a period of up to ninety years. If an elderly person remembers what a grandparent told him about what his grandparent had told him it is amazing how far back an oral account can go into the mists of time. In this collection of memories there is an account of how the news of victory at the Battle of Trafalgar was celebrated locally and so constitutes a living link back to an event over 200 years ago.

This oral history of Rawmarsh and Parkgate has focused especially on collecting information and opinions about the local area from the first sixty years of the twentieth century. By its very nature such an account may not be as factually accurate as a history based just on documentary evidence, as memories can become blurred over time. However, without recording these oral memories much of the information included here would have been lost, and that would have been a tragedy. In fact, many people retain very accurate memories of their younger days, even when they have reached their nineties. The oldest resident interviewed for this book was one month shy of her 100th birthday (and still went out to collect her newspaper every day, not to mention doing the crossword!).

Looking towards the old Manor House on High Street, *c.* 1908.

Rawmarsh and Parkgate are two small towns that have grown into one and are located close to the large town of Rotherham in South Yorkshire. Both communities have a fascinating history and an oral history record such as this must be one of the best ways of preserving memories of the changes in the towns. Despite being physically linked on the ground, it would be a grievous error to count Rawmarsh and Parkgate as one community. Time after time interviewees stressed their allegiance to either Rawmarsh or Parkgate, but not to both! Community identity is still very strong among older residents of the two towns, but apparently much less so among younger residents.

In all, nearly forty residents of Rawmarsh and Parkgate were interviewed for this book and most of these interviews were digitally recorded. I must stress my gratitude to all those who talked to me about their memories and welcomed me into their homes. It was an absolute delight to see their faces come alive as they recalled people and events from long ago. In most cases the same people provided photographs linked to their memories for me to copy, and once again I must thank them for their generosity and trust.

As a member of the Rawmarsh and Parkgate Local History Group I have been greatly assisted by those in the group who have allowed a 'foreigner', like myself from London, to share their interest and commitment to their local communities. (I have driven through Rawmarsh and Parkgate every working day for the last thirty-five years so I am not as foreign as I used to be!) As a teacher at St Pius X Catholic High School, close to Rawmarsh, I have been able to involve some students in the interviews. This has been part of the school's community outreach linked to history. Perhaps the funniest aspect of the project has been watching the students' faces, eyes wide and mouths gaping, as they listen to the childhood antics described by older and apparently respectable members of the community. Perhaps some things do not change with time as much as we might think! To illustrate this I have included just one newspaper extract along with all the oral memories right at the start of Chapter One. The extract is a letter from the 'Women of Parkgate'; it was written in 1914 and yet in many ways could just as easily have been written yesterday.

I hope the combined picture of Rawmarsh and Parkgate built up by all these interview extracts will inform the newer residents of the area and refresh the memories of the older residents. Although many memories of the past were shared by most interviewees, every single person provided some unique insights into the communities' history that might have been lost without this project. Hopefully other local people will read this book and decide to record their own memories; without doubt they too will provide further unique memories of the area's past. Most of the residents who were interviewed have very positive memories of the past, even though many of them grew up in a poverty younger people find hard to imagine. There were few holidays, fewer cars and virtually no telephones, yet people made their own entertainment and children generally roamed free and unfettered by parental concerns. They survived nights in the Anderson shelters, food rationing for years and teachers that used canes, and still apparently came out smiling. They worked in shops still open at eleven o'clock on a Saturday night, grabbed molten steel bars with metal tongs and lay on their sides mining coal with pick-axes, and still remained positive. There is certainly much in these collected memories to admire and much to inspire younger generations.

Anthony Dodsworth, 2009

one

EARLY MEMORIES

31 October 1914 – a letter from the women of Parkgate

Where is the Rawmarsh Urban District Council? There are many things in which at any rate the women of Parkgate would like it to give its attention. The men going to work spit all along the footpaths in a most disgusting manner. In a little while the children, many of them very small, walk along in this filth and carry it with them into school and home. Consumption is now a notifiable disease. Then why are the lads of any age up to sixteen

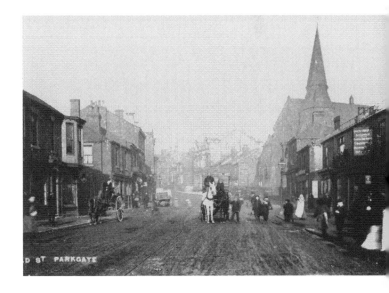

A view up Broad Street, showing the Methodist church at the end of Hollybush in the early 1900s.

or seventeen allowed to use the public streets in a most unashamed way as a lavatory? What about paper-throwing? Fried fish and chip bags, whole sheets of newspapers and innumerable other papers of all sizes, shapes and colour are thrown indiscriminately on the sidewalk and into people's gardens, while orange peel, banana skins etc are thrown down to the danger of pedestrians. Nobody seems to care. The children are allowed to chalk everyone's house and wall at their own sweet will. We know the schoolteachers have done, and are doing, their utmost to correct many of these evils, but the women of Parkgate think it is time for the Council to wake up and make by-laws and rigidly enforce them so teaching the inhabitants, and especially the rising generation, habits of self respect and – may we say it? – morality. We beg to remain, yours respectfully, The Women of Parkgate.

Rotherham Advertiser

Grandfather's memories

I talked to my grandfather quite a bit when I was young. Our family was linked with the Badger family in Rotherham, who were solicitors. We were also linked to the Pursglove and the Hawley families. Some of the Pursgloves were killed in the Warren Vale mining disaster of 1851.

My great-grandfather was arrested for poaching rabbits near Warren Vale once. He came to collect a rabbit caught in a snare and they were waiting for him. He was imprisoned in the Chapel on the Bridge in Rotherham for seven days.

My grandfather told me that his grandfather had sat him on his knee and told him about the celebrations in Swinton following the Battle of Trafalgar. The news arrived a couple of months after the battle itself and they had a big bonfire in the field behind the Gate Inn.

Harold Badger

Oxley's steelworks

The oldest part of the building at Oxley's had a big arch through it and there is a painting from 1835 showing it. I think it was one of the lodge gates for the Earl Fitzwilliam estate and that's what gave Parkgate its name.

In my day, as you approached the building the laboratory was on the left downstairs, with the offices above and the caretaker was on the right. The fettling went on through the arch. The yard there wasn't very big; two coal wagons would fill it. When they did some alterations to the building they uncovered a big chest with farm papers in it. There was something about the sale of a black mare and there were some papers linked to the transport of steel. The Board Room, or Director's Room, was also upstairs on the left and sometimes workers had lunch in there with the directors. There would be a proper cook in the room to serve the food. The old painting of the works used to hang up there.

George Hallam

A painting of Oxley's steelworks in 1835. Parts of the building survived until recently, but it has now all been demolished.

George Hallam receiving a long-service award on his retirement from Oxley's. He clocked up forty-one years, having started as a fettler in 1939. Note the painting in the background.

Silver City

We lived in Rosehill Road, Rawmarsh, when I was a girl. It was the top road of a group of houses built by John Brown & Co. for their work people, who were mostly miners. It went by the name of 'Silver City' because at the time it was being built there was a Gold Rush to a region of the Yukon Territory in Canada called 'The Klondike' (1897-1898) and some of the locals used to call it 'The Klondike'. Most people in Rawmarsh call it 'T'city'. It was a very friendly place, self-contained. You didn't have to go anywhere else for shopping if you didn't want to, although a lot of people shopped at the Co-op, which was in Main Street, Ryecroft, just across the road from T'city. In T'city there were four shops; two were general stores and one was a butcher's shop, which was owned by a Mrs Davis, who was the butcher. Her husband worked in the offices at Aldwarke coal mine. It didn't matter what you went to the butcher's for, there was always a ha'porth over. Mrs Davis became known as the 'ha'porth over butcher'. She also went by the name of 'Aunty Minnie'.

Elsie Beaumont

My family roots

I was born in 1923 in South Street and later moved to Marrion Road and then Dale Road. My dad worked for the Co-op in Parkgate. I went to Rosehill School and then was one of the first pupils to go through Haugh Road Secondary School. I sang in the choir at the chapel in Ryecroft from being about sixteen years old.

I found out that my grandfather, Charles Bray [born 1856], moved to Parkgate from Great Snoring in north Norfolk. He was brought to Parkgate as a boy by his parents Charles William Bray and Susan Bray [*née* Thompson]. Grandad was a Methodist preacher and helped to set up the Bethel Chapel in Lloyd Street, Parkgate, being one of the trustees. My grandad had four brothers and a sister and one of the brothers, William

Cyril Bray on an eightieth birthday outing to the North York Moors Railway.

John Bray, was recorded in the 1871 Census as living with his parents and employed as a solicitor's clerk. In 1876 he sailed from Gravesend to Australia as a Methodist missionary. Having left Parkgate, William found life hard out in Australia and he died in 1897 at the age of forty-two. I have now made contact with his family in Australia.

Cyril Bray

Rockcliffe House

My family were the Willeys, who ended up living in Rockcliffe House at the top of Rawmarsh Hill. William Willey, following in the footsteps of his father and grandfather, became a master butcher and in 1868 established his own business at 8 Broad Street. He married Mary Naylor, daughter of a local coal merchant, and they set up their first home above the shop.

William prospered and eventually bought land opposite the parish church to build a larger, roomy house with outbuildings. By 1897 the house was finished and William moved his wife and children into their new home. There was ample room for the two servants to live in and there was an airy, modern kitchen. There were three large rooms downstairs – a very large dining room, a large lounge and a library – along with the kitchen and a scullery. There were six bedrooms upstairs with a very well arranged bathroom with a step to

The Willey family outside Rockcliffe House, *c.* 1900. One of the family was added later to the photograph.

The wedding of Amy Willey and Edward Hulbert, shown outside Rockcliffe House in 1906.

climb into the bath. There were bells in the kitchen for every room. The library was used as a study by William. Each year there were so many for Christmas dinner that, despite a long dining table, they had to have two sittings and there were three maids to serve them. Outside the house there were stables for the horse and carriage, outbuildings for storage, space for an orchard, a large vegetable garden, a paddock and a meadow stretching down to a tributary of the River Don, perfect for the sheep and cattle held in transit. William also owned some houses across the road. William and Mary slept in a four-poster bed and on Sunday evening the family gathered together in the house to listen to the church bells ringing across the road.

In June 1899, when William and Mary celebrated their thirtieth wedding anniversary, all the family gathered together for a special meal and had a family portrait taken. William's son Willie couldn't get leave from the butcher's shop in Sheffield where he was working, so when the photographer arranged the group he left a space on the back row to insert his image later.

June Roberts

Like Dodge City

My Grandad Brown told me when I was young (he always called me 'm'lad') that his parents had come from Bromsgrove, in Worcestershire, to Parkgate. When he arrived from Bromsgrove he got a job at the steelworks and ended up as a blacksmith there. He used to tell me that Parkgate was like Dodge City when he was growing up at the end of the 1890s. There were problems because youths were getting money from working in the steelworks and the pits to spend on drink and often they had moved into Parkgate for work without any family. They were drunk going to work sometimes and there were more than twenty pubs in Parkgate and Rawmarsh. There were no restrictions on opening hours then. They got into fights, they spent time winding up the police and ended up behind bars. My grandad was a real Victorian; he thought women should be kept in their place. He never went to any of the family weddings. He used to say if you want to keep your wife safe when you go out, put her hair in the mangle!

Malcolm Brown

Rawmarsh before the First World War

Another thing I remember about Rawmarsh is the number of yards there were. There was Adams Yard, Pump Yard, Holmes Yard, Pottery Yard, Cope's Yard, Spick's Yard, Neville's Yard, Moxon's Yard, Lilley's Yard and Craven Yard. All the yards seemed to have their own peculiarity. I can remember Lilley's Yard having 'Ant Omi'; I think her name was Naomi and everyone called her auntie, so she always went by the name 'Ant Omi'. There was also Providence Place, which was a very pleasant cul-de-sac.

At that time Rawmarsh had a very good prize band. In the Star Inn yard there was a sort of underground place that went into Stocks Lane and on Sunday mornings the band used to practise there. It was the custom for people to gather in the Star Inn yard to listen to the band practising.

Before the First World War, Westfield Road was called 'New Begin'. It was only a narrow lane with a few cottages at the Greasbrough Road end and one largish house where Newbould, the pit manager, lived. At the top of 'New Begin' there was a spring where animals used to stop for a drink on their way from the market. At that time farmers used to buy their cattle at Rotherham market and walk them home to the various farms around here. Sometimes there would be stray animals, so there was a small closed-in piece of ground near the spring called 'The Pinfold'. Stray animals were fastened in there until they were claimed.

Elsie Beaumont

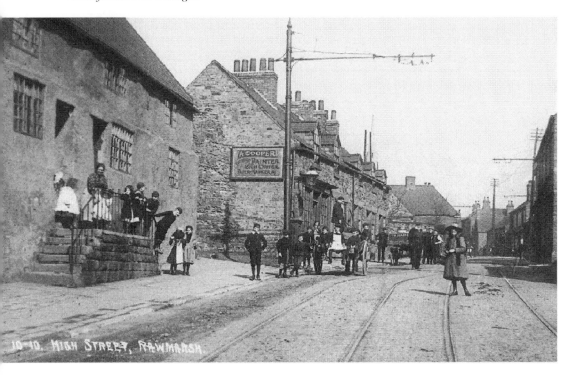

High Street early in the twentieth century. Note the tram tracks are in place.

Norfolk roots

My grandfather and his four brothers came to Rotherham around 1890 from Weasenham All Saints in Norfolk in search of work. Later he was joined by my grandmother and they were married at Rawmarsh Parish Church. They settled at a house in France Street (which is still there) where my father, the eldest of four children, was born. Before the war we holidayed in Norfolk, staying with Auntie Lottie and Uncle Bob in their farm labourer's cottage with no running water but a pump in the garden. We travelled by train from Parkgate, eventually arriving at the Swanton Morley Junction, where Uncle Bob was awaiting us with a pony and cart in which to complete the journey. We enjoyed visits to Fakenham and Cromer on the days when the ramshackle bus passed through the village. Uncle Bob worked on the farm and I remember him bringing in a rabbit which he had caught and rabbit pie was served up for lunch the following day (Ugh!). He was also a local preacher, cycling many miles each Sunday to conduct worship at one of the many small village chapels. They were happy days.

Marian Overland

Left: William and Lucy Overland, the grandfather and grandmother of Marian Overland. They migrated to Parkgate from Norfolk around 1890.

Below: Leonard Schonhut, a well-known character in Parkgate who ran a successful butcher's business from his shop in Broad Street.

The Schonhut connection

Leonard Schonhut owned the top shop in Parkgate. It was a really big business; it had a big wholesale business as well as the shop. They made bread, pastries and pies. There was a slaughterhouse out the back and the pigs were brought in from the Schonhuts' farms near Selby. I was related to the Schonhuts by marriage. Grandpa and Grandma Schonhut first came over to England from Germany around 1880 and settled down in Dore. They had twelve children and Grandpa Schonhut made sure all the boys were set up as butchers in their own shops and all the girls' husbands likewise. That was how Leonard got his shop. Several of the family had problems during the First World War because of their German name. Some of the shops were attacked after the sinking of the *Lusitania* and at least two of the Schonhuts changed their names.

Schonhut's 'top' shop on Broad Street with staff members standing outside.

Schonhut's top shop is still there, but now it is a florist. It is just across from the Clarence, opposite the Yorkshire Bank. There are two red marble columns at the entrance like there used to be when it was Schonhut's.

Malcolm Brown

My early days in Parkgate

I was born at 36 Greasbrough Road, Parkgate, in 1898. It was an old terrace house where the only light was the glow of a paraffin lamp. The toilets were down the garden path: two holes next to each other over a midden. The midden was emptied and cleaned out every fortnight by the night-soil men. Then men had to barrow the silt up the garden path, through the entrance and on to the road. It was then carted away and the road was disinfected.

My father and my grandfather were miners at Aldwarke Main and Roundwood Colliery and the top wage then was about 3s a day. Later we moved to 41 France Street and there

Leslie Evans as a young man. Life was hard for him growing up in Parkgate.

we had our first gas light with a mantle. The rent was 5*s* a week and our meal most days was either a rabbit or an oxtail which cost 6*d* each.

Leslie Evans

Mother's help with making poggies

My great-grandma, Mrs Glossop, lived on Dale Road, opposite Low Pottery. My mother told me that she used to help her to make 'poggies' to put in kettles to keep them free of lime. She helped with the thimbling and got a ha'porth of toffee from her grandma. She used to fetch clay from the pottery and then work the clay through a tube to get it near the right size. They would roll the clay in their hands and produce balls of clay about double the size of a Malteser. The poggies were first used in the kilns to separate plates as they were fired and then, once taken from between the plates, were used in kettles.

John Turner

Fire!

There used to be two flat-roofed shops in front of Sunnyside Cottage right beside the old High Street. They disappeared when they widened the road. My mother had them built by Pugh's. My mother sold greengroceries, bouquets and wreaths in one of the shops. She was up at six to go to the market and opened the shop at nine. It stayed open till eight at night. The other shop she let to a woman who sold little children's clothes like boys' romper suits. She also sold knitting wools and patterns. It had been a hairdresser's once and after that it was a sweet shop run by a Mr Gregory. You could get mint imperials for a ha'penny a quarter. This would have been well before the war.

Just to the right of these shops was another with a parapet decorated with mosaic. Tom Ward owned that shop. One night my mother looked out the window and saw the shop on fire. It was in October and I think it was about 1906. They had all the fireworks in the shop for Bonfire Night was coming up. The woman who ran the shop tried to get the shop takings from a drawer at the bottom of a wardrobe and pulled it over on top of her. She managed to get out with her two or three girls and my mother had to give them some clothes because they had no clothes. My grandfather, Tom, was really angry; it wasn't long before he died. The fire brigade was pulled by horses and when the horses got to the big horse trough near the top of Rawmarsh Hill, where the War Memorial is now, the lead fireman ordered them to stop and get a drink and this was only 100 yards away from the fire. My grandfather created a fuss about it because there were the horses drinking just down the road from where the shop was blazing away.

Mary Ferns

Rawmarsh Church.

St Mary's Church with the horse trough below it where the fire engine halted while Tom Ward's shop burned.

Celebrating New Year's Eve

New Year's Eve was a very enjoyable time. We always had a Watchnight Service and afterwards we used to stand outside the church and sing carols. It was traditional that all the pubs turned out at midnight and joined us. I remember how well we used to sing 'Hail Smiling Morn' and 'How Beautiful upon the Mountains'. Sadly all this has passed away, but I do have happy memories of those days up to the beginning of the First World War. Things seemed to change after that.

Elsie Beaumont

Traffic accident on Rawmarsh High Street

My Auntie, Cathy Ward, was rather accident-prone. One day she took the horse and cart out of our house on the High Street, Sunnyside, and it rushed straight out onto the road. It just missed the up-tram, but collided with the down-tram. This would have been before 1910. My mother told me the traffic manager came up from the tram sheds to see them and there was an exchange of letters. Auntie Cathy worked in the women's gowns department at Kilnhurst Co-op. Eventually, she got killed by a car at the bottom of Rawmarsh.

Mary Ferns

Trams in the tram sheds on Dale Road. Cathy Ward was in collision with one of these while on her horse and cart.

Zeppelin raid on Ryecroft

We bought our house in Kilnhurst Road from Mrs Marshall and she told us about the time the area was bombed in the First World War. It is mentioned in Rosehill School's logbook. On Sunday 25 September 1917 there was a Zeppelin raid at night and a bomb was dropped on the field next to Rosehill School and it blew out a lot of the windows around here. Despite this, the following morning the children had to go to school – my mother was one of those – but had to wear their overcoats as there were no windows! The bomb hole was there right through to the 1960s when Bradlea Rise was built.

Frank Horner

The bottom end of Warren Vale

My grandfather, Harry Hill, and grandmother lived on the corner of the road up to Piccadilly and Warren Vale. Their house was in a field close to a row of cottages called Pinch Row. It was an old house with big, thick walls and a big beam running across the main room ceiling. They used to have to use paraffin lamps for lighting. I can always remember they had a horse-hair couch under the window; it used to tickle my legs. There was a pump on the sink to get water from. The well was further up the yard. They had a big, black, iron kettle that was always steaming on the kitchen range. You went down a few steps to the kitchen and it had a flagged floor.

The Sellars lived further up the hill and on the opposite side, near where the tram crashed, were the Froggatts in a stone cottage and nearby there were two brick semis. There was Mrs Needham's little sweet shop close as well.

Just up the road to Warren House, on the left, there was another house. They used to go hawking from there, selling things like paraffin. My grandfather was a woodman on the Wentworth estate. He originated from Lincolnshire and had previously lived at Lea

Marjorie Oxer's grandfather, Harry Hill, who lived in a cottage on Warren Vale close to the old toll bar.

The site of a tram crash that happened on Warren Vale in July 1908, close to Harry Hill's cottage.

Brook. I thought it was a wonderful place to visit, with all the space in the field round the house and the pigs and the chickens there as well. I wasn't so keen on the earth closets though!

They used to pay the rent every six months and they would take their pony and trap out to visit the estate office in Wentworth to pay. Sometimes they took me with them and I can remember they always gave us a meal in the stable block and it was served on wooden plates. Grandfather also had a horse and cart for his work. They got their water from a well near the house, but if it ran dry they would collect water instead from the drift. You had to cross the road and go into the plantation to get there. You climbed over a fence and dropped right down to a stream. The house that stood above this area (and is still there) was split into two and the Carrs lived there. The Pinch Row houses faced up towards Rawmarsh. The Webbs were one of the families that lived in them.

Marjorie Oxer

Gleaning the fields

When they took in the harvest near Greasbrough Tops my dad used to say, 'They're cutting the last today so I'll take you up.' We used to sit and watch. When they started on the last bit of the harvest in the middle of the field all the rabbits ran out and they were shot. They always used to give my dad a rabbit. We used to go up after they had finished and collect the gleanings, the seeds that were left on the ground. We would bring a bag home and then

A view from Greasbrough Tops looking towards Church Street and showing the fields where Edna Vaughan went gleaning when she was young.

sit outside sorting the wheat from the chaff by blowing gently through our hands. Then we half filled two of those stone jars with wheat and filled them up with water. We would put them in the oven overnight because the coal fire was kept in all night. In the morning there used to be a thick film on top – you could put your finger through it. We used to put it in a dish and open a tin of Nestle's milk, pour it on and mix it up. That was our breakfast, it was delicious. My dad used to call it 'frummety'.

Edna Vaughan

Growing up

I can recall my father bringing me to see my aunt in Queen's Street after a bomb had been dropped in the field next to Rosehill School. It broke a lot of the windows in the street. Generally we weren't well off enough to have holidays till I was quite grown up. I can remember going to Bournemouth then and that was by coach.

We grew up living near the Electra Picture Palace. On Saturday nights people used to queue right past our house. There were two houses in the same complex; one was occupied by the caretaker and the other by Mr Amphlett, who used to play the piano for the silent films. On Saturday afternoons the children could go to a matinee. It cost *2d* for the best seats upstairs and 1*d* for the cheap seats downstairs. I used to have 3*d* to spend, 2*d* to go in the best seats and a penny I used to spend in a shop opposite that sold newspapers, biscuits and sweets. You could buy a bar of Cadbury's chocolate then for a penny. In those days it was not wrapped, you just had it put in a paper bag. They also had toffee on a tray which they would break up with a little hammer.

Living in Parkgate, I didn't used to come up to Rawmarsh very often at all, just to the park really. I do remember my father taking me to Wentworth House once on a Boxing Day to see the Hunt setting off. There were all the dogs and horses there, but then the meet had to be cancelled because there had been too much snow.

Nellie Schofield

Grandma's house on Victoria Road

On Victoria Road there was a shop called Geeson's and my Grandma Hawley lived next door. My grandma's house had been a pub. It had been called the Victoria Tavern and it was run by Mr and Mrs Booth. For some reason the tavern was known locally as the Birdcatchers. It was converted into two houses and my grandma's had a big cellar with boxes in the wall to put bottles in. My father played for the football team there; they were called the Blood Tubs. You knew what to expect when you played there! I remember my grandma's front room was full of silverware, I think from Rotherham Harriers.

My grandad's brother was called Harry Hawley and he was a runner. My father told me that the bookies took hold of Harry and took him to Edinburgh to compete in the Powderhall Sprints over 110 yards. I think he won it and the bookies made a bit of a killing. Harry and my Aunt Alma had a newsagent's shop on Aldwarke Lane. The Hawleys have always been good runners. Earl Fitzwilliam used to hold a gala at Wentworth every year and my Aunts Blanche and Eadie used to run in everything and win all the prizes. Eventually it was decided to ban them because they always won!

Cliff Hawley

Life in Parkgate

Grandma and Grandpa Lowry lived on Netherfield Lane. Grandpa had come from Ireland to work in the pits. Grandpa Owens came to Parkgate from Wales via Broseley near Ironbridge. They lived close to Victoria Road too.

I don't remember any soup kitchens or anything like that in the General Strike of 1926, but people did used to go down to a stream at Aldwarke and dig some coal out there.

The Lowry family on holiday in Blackpool. Some of the family worked in hotels there.

The stream used to run between the two bridges and out into the Meadows. I don't remember going hungry; there was always bread and jam or bread and dripping. My dad was a miner then, so he was out on strike. Later he lost his job and that was when I got him a job at the steelworks. We did used to get a bit of begging, perhaps, from other people in the street and when my dad did get coal they tried to get some of that.

Henry Lowry

Herbal remedies

My dad, Edward Jones, had books full of information about herbs and upstairs in our attic he had three big tin trunks full of herbs. We used to go out and collect all these herbs and put them in little bags, one for each herb. Then the bags were put in the trunks. When someone used to come to us looking for a herb to make up a medicine, dad would go up and get it from the trunk. You didn't go to doctors generally because it cost you money. Eventually the family passed on all his herbalist books to Tommy Tildesley and he became famous for his medicines. I can remember making up a mixture of liquorice and sulphur, used for clearing you out! One day I got a message from the boys' teacher at Kilnhurst Road asking me to refrain from giving the boys liquorice and sulphur as the class couldn't

An advertisement for Tommy Tildesley's shop on Broad Street, highlighting his numerous herbal products.

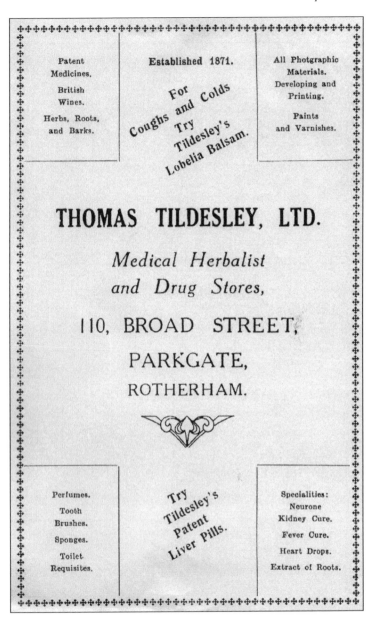

stand it! My dad used to use liquorice and linseed for coughs. He used to get those big sticks of liquorice. He also used vinegar, butter and sugar for sore throats and coughs. I don't think anyone ever gave him any money for the herbs and medicines he provided. I used to make pills out of powder that dad gave me and put them into boxes.

Edna Vaughan

Early years on Aldwarke Road

My father was Edward Bancroft and he was a boiler maker at Parkgate Iron and Steel Works up to the age of sixty-five, when he retired. He had started as an apprentice at Mexborough Plant and moved to Parkgate when he finished his apprenticeship. Then he lived in lodgings in Pottery Street. He married my mother, who came from Conisbrough. Her father was a farm labourer who moved around different farms, whoever wanted to hire him. We lived on Aldwarke Road in a terraced house close to the Electra Cinema. I remember an old gentleman, and I mean old, who lived in the buildings linked with Aldwarke Hall, who used to be driven by Mr Town in a horse and trap to a gentlemen's club over a bank on Rawmarsh Hill. It was just below where the library is. The name of the old man was Mr Thirkell. He had an adopted son. The stables at the hall had been made into cottages at that time and they had stone-flagged floors downstairs. We used to have no bathroom, so the big iron bath was kept in the cellar and brought out when someone needed a bath. The water would be heated up in the copper and put into the bath in front of the kitchen hearth. We didn't have a bathroom until we came to live in Ryecroft.

Nellie Schofield

The Bank House is shown in the centre of this photograph, which was where Mr Thirkell attended a gentlemen's club on the first floor of the building.

The old Poor House

When I was young I can remember visiting my Uncle Colin Lilley in the old Poor House; he lived there with his wife Agnes and brought up thirteen children there. Its address was 1 Workhouse Buildings, Lilley's Yard and was on the High Street, nearly opposite Pottery Street. It was the building that had been used in Rawmarsh as the workhouse before the big one was built in Rotherham in the 1830s.

My grandparents lived in the Poor House. Samuel Lilley came from Dudley and worked in coal mines from the age of nine to sixty-nine. Fifty-three of those years he worked in the Stubbin Collieries. He married Eliza Marshall and they had sixteen children, two of whom died very young. I don't know where all the children fitted in the house! Samuel and Eliza were married at Greasbrough in 1873 and celebrated their diamond wedding in 1933, a rare event then. Samuel was said to have been very strong and, as well as being a miner, he kept pigs.

Joan Pearce

Left: The old Poor House building on High Street that became the home for the Lilley family.
Right: Samuel and Eliza Lilley, who raised fourteen children in the old Poor House building and celebrated their diamond wedding in 1933.

The almhouses on Dale Road that were built with money provided by the Goodwin Trust.

The almshouses

There used to be three little almshouses on Dale Road with just two rooms each: a bedroom and a living place. They were little cottages that belonged to the church. The only people who could live in them were widows. The almshouses were built close to the old boys' grammar school.

Betty Watts

Nocturnal wanderings

Walking at night was a great pastime as you could really depend on the weather, not like now. We walked right up Cortworth Lane, past Elsecar Reservoir and back up Botley Bank, calling at a few orchards for a few windfalls to eat on the way.

Some of the girls who we were knocking about with went to work at Blackpool or St Anne's and it was a problem getting to see them, but we soon solved it. We used to buy a pocket watch from Seniors at a bob a week, take it next door and pawn it for thirty bob. The train fare to Blackpool was 5*s* 9*d* return so two of us were okay off with a bit of spendo. All that way for a wrestle on the sand hills!

Jim Evans

Working during the General Strike

When I was young, around 1920, all the land beyond Claypit Lane was fields; there were no houses there then. There was a farm at the top of the hill. That was where they had a soup kitchen for poor people during the General Strike. My dad was a miner; he had some work during the strike because he was a 'bobby' on the tip heap at Aldwarke Main to stop people digging for coal there. Both his brothers were miners at that time and they had no work.

Muriel Sykes

Settling in Ryecroft

When I was young I lived in South Street in Ryecroft and we were there till we moved in 1939. We lived at 75 and my grandma at 87. We had relatives living at 85 as well. For a long time there were just those two houses on one side at the bottom of South Street; my grandad, had them built and originally my great-grandfather, John Edward Caroline, lived in one. He came from Belper originally and he worked in the mines like my grandad. Grandad used to work at Warren House Colliery. My grandma was a Brameld and was linked to the Bramelds at Rockingham Pottery. The Brameld family had a connection with Butterbusk Farm near Conisbrough. They [the houses] were probably built about 1885. When my grandma and grandad first went to live there, they used to get their water from a well at the bottom of the garden. They used to come and examine it during the war to make sure it still had water in it.

Freda Stacey

two

SCHOOLDAYS

Half-time certificate

At the age of eleven I got a job on a milk round; the wages were 2s per week and I had to get up at six o'clock in the morning. First I had to change a horse from a Royal Mail cart to a milk float and then go alone and fetch 40 gallons of milk from a farm at Greasbrough, getting back at about eight o'clock. The milk was then carried in 2-gallon cans; I myself carried two, one with a pint ladle and the other with a gill ladle. I served the nearest customers first as the farthest lived about two miles away. I arrived home about half-past twelve, in time to go to school in the afternoon. To be allowed to do this I had to have a half-time certificate, granted by the school governors.

Leslie Evans

Paper round before school

I passed the scholarship to go to Mexborough Grammar in 1924 when I was twelve. My dad was working in the pit at the time. Dad went to see the headmaster, Clem White, and decided I couldn't go, but Mr White said he would help me anyway with work and things. Dad couldn't afford to lose my 4s a week for my paper round. I used to do miles every morning, covering Parkgate and Rawmarsh. I started my round by six o'clock on Terrace Road, down Ashwood Road, up Bear Tree Road, back to Aldwarke Road, then up to France Street, Greasbrough Hill up to the vicarage, back up Holm Flatt Street, up past

The Parkgate Midland railway station from which many local people set off for day trips and holidays.

the duck pond on Westfield Road, then Blythe Avenue, West Avenue, East Avenue, then past the tram sheds into Claypit Lane and up into Green Lane. It used to take me about two hours. If I was late for school after that I'd get the stick. I also sold the Green 'Un on Saturday evening at Four Lane Ends. I got tuppence ha'penny a dozen for those I sold and I used to sell about fourteen dozen. We used to collect them from down at the railway station. The Hawleys were the newsagents I worked for. I remember Fred Hawley from when I was young; he was one of the best half-milers in the country.

Henry Lowry

Started at Christ Church School

I went to Christ Church School first, but a bit later I went on to Ashwood Road. I can remember the teachers at Christ Church all wore big black aprons to keep the chalk dust off their clothes. My sister stopped at Christ Church till she was fourteen, but I was moved because Ashwood Road was considered a superior school. After that I passed the scholarship and went on to Wath Grammar School. I was there when the new building was finished, but most of it has been knocked down now.

Nellie Schofield

The interior of Christ Church on Aldwarke Road. The school Nellie Schofield attended briefly was next door.

Saving with the Penny Bank

I was born in 1926 in Aldwarke Road in Parkgate. My grandfather and grandmother, Mr and Mrs Dewick, ran the fish and chip shop opposite the Electra cinema and I was born there. Not long afterwards we moved to Hollybush Street and then to East Avenue when I was nearly two. My father was a blacksmith at the Chemical Works. I went to school first at Main Street (Miss I'Anson was the headmistress – she was lovely) and then on to Rosehill. I can remember when it was George V's Silver Jubilee in 1935 that if children opened an account with the Yorkshire Penny Bank in school 1s was put into the account by the government to celebrate the event. The shilling had to stay in your account until you left school and mine is still in! I wonder what it's worth now. We carried on saving through school and drew money out if me and mum went to Cleethorpes for a little holiday or to buy a few things for Christmas.

Edna Pease

Celebrating the coronation of King George VI

To commemorate the coronation of George VI and Queen Elizabeth an afternoon of celebration in Rosehill Park was arranged by Rawmarsh Urban District Council. It began with a service around the bandstand attended by councillors, ministers and all sections of the public. After this, a tree-planting ceremony took place in which one child from each school planted a copper beech tree circling the bandstand. I was elected to represent Netherfield Lane School – I think because most of the children knew me as I was a 'milk monitor' and collected their ha'penny daily for the morning bottle of milk. There followed a full programme of races – egg and spoon, wheelbarrow and three-legged – in sections for primary, junior and secondary. The friendly rivalry was enjoyed by all. As a keepsake of the coronation, every child within the West Riding Authority was presented with a specially produced silver spoon and a pen.

Marian Overland

3.15 p.m. CEREMONY OF TREE PLANTING.

COPPER BEECH TREES will be planted in a portion of the Park allocated for the purpose, which in future will be known as the "CORONATION BOWER."

TREES will be planted by the following :—

Chairman of the Council.

Arthur Gordon James representing Rawmarsh Senior School Boys.

Blanche Fletcher	representing Rawmarsh Senior School Girls.
John Roberts	representing Rawmarsh Ashwood Senior School Boys.
Phyllis Jones	representing Rawmarsh Ashwood Senior School Girls.
Marian Overland	representing Rawmarsh Netherfield Lane School Junior Mixed.
Edward Fernley	representing Rawmarsh Netherfield Lane School Infants.
George Wilfred Briggs	representing Rawmarsh Ryecroft School Infants.
James Roe	representing Rawmarsh Rosehill Council Junior Mixed.
Anthony Knutton	representing Rawmarsh Rotherham Road School Infants.
Brian David Hillier	representing Rawmarsh Haugh Council Junior Mixed and Infants.
Cornelius Turner	representing Rawmarsh Parkgate Council Junior Boys.
Marie Thorpe	representing Rawmarsh Parkgate Council Junior Girls.
Jack Wadsworth	representing Rawmarsh Parkgate Council Infants.
Eric Poole	representing Rawmarsh C. of E. Junior Boys.
Jean Goss	representing Rawmarsh C. of E. Junior Girls.
Albert Hanson	representing Rawmarsh C. of E. Infants.
Josephine Evans	representing Rawmarsh St. Joseph's Roman Catholic Junior Mixed and Infants.

A list of pupils from schools in Rawmarsh and Parkgate who planted trees in Rosehill Park to celebrate the coronation of King George VI.

Rosehill Hall, at the heart of Rosehill Park, where the copper beeches were planted.

Friday afternoon treat

Bobby Hanley was a school bobby, I can remember. He was ex-army and he wore a bowler hat and had a waxed moustache. John Cater was the headmaster at Dale Road. Mr Teal was also there; he was a tough teacher. When he went into the classroom the first thing he did was to take his cane out of his desk. The cane had black tape round it. He did teach about the war while it was happening, things like what was happening and where. He loved reading to us and if we had been good, on a Friday afternoon he would put on his pince-nez and read to us from *Children of the New Forest* or *Oliver Twist*. If we hadn't been good we did maths. I can remember him going into the 'poor cupboard' to find clothes and shoes for some of the poorest children.

Ron Liversidge

What the Dickens!

My brother used to play cricket for Christ Church and their field was up near the vicarage on the road across to Greasbrough. I went with my mother and father to watch them play. We got a lift up to the pitch on one of the charabancs from Faulkner's.

A crowd across the end of Hall Street, Parkgate, which probably gathered at a nearby soup kitchen during the 1926 General Strike.

I went to the Bethel Chapel in Lloyd Street. I went first with one of my friends, who was a Methodist. I went there till it closed and then I moved across to the Wesleyan chapel on Broad Street.

I can remember the General Strike in 1926 when so many people were out of work. During the strike my father went to work on a farm so he could get some money. I think the churches arranged soup kitchens at that time.

My teachers at Ashwood Road seemed to think my family was a bit better off than most, but I don't know why. I think we were always nicely dressed and my mother kept us clean. My mother was a dressmaker before she got married, so she could sew. Once we were reading *David Copperfield* at school and we hadn't enough books to go round, so three girls were having to sit together and share. I had a copy at home and the teacher thought that was wonderful; I took it into school so that made one more! One of my teachers at Ashwood Road was Miss Parkin and the teacher we had in the top class was very strict, but I always said she was the best teacher I ever had. Another of the teachers was a Miss Lee and she lived in Greasbrough; her brother was a local preacher. There was also Miss Headworth, I remember her because she also went to the Bethel.

Later, when I went to Wath Grammar School, I had to catch a tram. I got a double-decker up to the Woodman and then a single-decker down to the school. I can remember making the journey before the new road was built on Warren Vale and on more than one occasion the Wath Grammar children had to get off the tram to allow it to get up the hill. It would get so far up the hill and run back down – then we knew we had to get off! My friend, Mrs

A tram at the foot of Rawmarsh Hill. Nellie Schofield caught a tram to get her to secondary school.

Carr, went with me to Ashwood Road and then to Wath. Now we are both ninety-four and we still talk to each other on the phone. She lives in Park Road.

Nellie Schofield

Good but strict

I started school at South Street and then went on to Rosehill when I was seven. They built air-raid shelters at South Street School in 1939 and they were there for a long time after the war. We used to plant our bulbs in there where it was dark. I started in Miss Firkins' class and I can remember after dinner you had to put your head down on the table and try to go to sleep, although I never managed it. Some schools even had beds for their youngest children. After that I had Miss Pepper, Miss Marshall and Miss Hayward. Miss I'Anson was the headmistress at Ryecroft and we thought she was very posh because she had a car.

When I went on to Rosehill I had Mrs Reeve (she was allowed to teach because she was a widow and there was a shortage of teachers in wartime), Miss Cranidge (who had to retire because she had TB) and Mr Skeldon. Mr Ingham was the headmaster there, he was good but strict. It was a very good school and children came from all over because it had a good reputation for getting children through the scholarship. I can remember children came from Swinton.

A view of children surrounding a maypole in Ryecroft in the first part of the twentieth century.

I got the stick once at school from Miss Roebuck, for rubbing a hole in my paper when I was trying to draw a horse's head. It was wartime and you had to be really careful with any materials. I was never an artist, but both my mum and my dad were.

Freda Stacey

Growing up

I went to the old Church of England school on Dale Road and we lived close by on Peashill Street. The street was all terraced houses, but one side was much older than the other. The newer side were built around 1910 and that's where I lived. The older ones were smaller and built around the 1870s; they were blackened with smoke. They've been knocked down now. My memories of school were not very happy. They used the cane a lot whether you had done something wrong or not.

My Auntie Annie and her husband George ran Roe's Farm on Dale Road and my father used to take the milk out for them to sell. (At times my father was hired out as a farm labourer at the Statutes Fair in October in Rotherham. That's what he did before he joined the army in the First World War. He had a hard life looking back at it.) They had about ten cows in the field at the front of the house. My aunt used to come to the railings and bring me sweets when I was going to school.

Reg Ferns

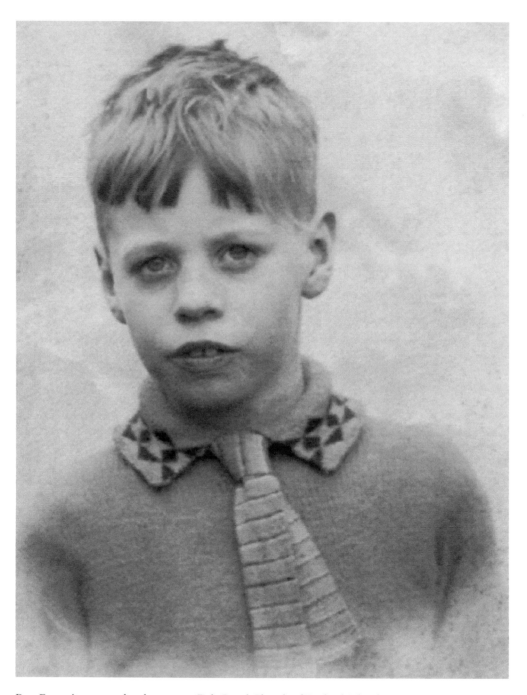

Reg Ferns. As a young boy he went to Dale Road Church of England School.

Playing truant

I didn't care for school at all, I couldn't accept it. I played truant from school as much as I could. I can remember one time playing on the Hollow by Infirmary Road, damming up a little rivulet with grass sods and being grabbed by 'Bobby Hanley' round the neck. He was the school 'bobby' and had been a captain in the army during the war. He used to wear a bowler hat. I used to do a runner with our Doreen, my sister, who was eighteen months younger than me. She was good at learning. She was in my class and knew all the answers, so we used to copy off her. We used to climb over the gate, but she didn't really want to come. There was a little group of boys who used to take off with us; there was Charlie Sykes, Reggie Clark and Dennis Roberts. We used to hang around Schonhut's abattoir near Bear Tree Road and ask for pigs' bladders to use as footballs.

I went to Netherfield Lane School first and then Ashwood Road. Mr Pengelly ran the football team at Netherfield Lane and him and me used to pick the team. I used to go to training with Rotherham United on Wednesday nights. Mr Pengelly used to give me a ha'penny for the bus fare and I joined up with about four other Rawmarsh lads to go to Millmoor sometimes.

The boys and girls were taught separately at Ashwood Road and I can remember that there were like army huts in the yard, one for teaching woodwork and one for metalwork. There was no playing field so we used to play on the Rec.

Cliff Hawley

Living Treasure Island

When I was four years four months old – September 1931 – my mum took me to school at Netherfield Lane. We queued in the corridor and there was a teacher sitting at a very high desk on a very high chair. My mother gave her my details and I went into the baby class. The teacher was Miss Askew. This was the only time my mother came to school. My brother, Raymond, would bring me home at twelve o'clock, take me back at half-past one and bring me home again at four o'clock. He was two and a half years older than me. In the baby class there was a very big old-fashioned rocking horse.

We had outside toilets and a school yard for PT and games. When I got to the top class Mr Pengelly was our teacher, a very dedicated teacher, and every Friday afternoon after playtime he used to read us *Treasure Island* and believe me he lived it. He always got a bit carried away.

We had a May Day every year at Netherfield Lane School; we were all attendants with lovely long white dresses. My Auntie Nellie made my long white dress.

Some of the young children who attended Netherfield Lane School in 1932, including Joan Gillions.

I moved up to Haugh Road. It was a new school; it had only been built two years before – built in a sort of a square with a quadrangle in the middle covered with a big grass lawn. We had a lovely big school field and inside toilets – sheer luxury! The boys' and girls' departments were separate from each other. School dinners were 4*d* in old money, but mother could not afford this so again we walked home for dinner and back for half-past one. We thought nothing of it because we were so used to walking everywhere.

I was in the netball team and the rounders team; we used to play other schools and we felt very important. I also did a lot of swimming and got all sorts of certificates and medals. We were very fortunate at Rawmarsh because Rawmarsh Baths were built in 1926 so that the coal miners could have baths and not go home dirty.

Joan Gillions

Delivering eggs

I was born and brought up on Church Street. Our house was around the middle of the street, one of the eight back-to-back houses there that were classified as slums. Our house was at the back and joined up to my grandad and grandma's house. The Liversidge family, who were relatives of ours, lived next door. I had a wonderful time down there, the people

If the cap fits! Ted Frost
grew up on Church Street.

were really friendly. If you were in the street and you were thirsty you could pop into anyone's house and they would give you a drink. My mother rented some land on the allotments at the top of the street and used to keep chickens. My Uncle Horace, next door, helped my mum with the chickens. I used to deliver the eggs to Greasbrough and I got a penny a time for doing so. I used to enjoy getting over the stream that comes down from

New Stubbin pit. There was a rope there attached to a tree and I used to swing across the stream like Tarzan. I never broke any of the eggs doing this.

I started school at Netherfield Lane and then on to Ashwood Road. I finished off at Haugh Road. I didn't really like it at Haugh Road. My dad was a strict disciplinarian. He had a belt and if there was any trouble he'd say, 'It's coming off' and we'd all go quiet. You couldn't eat away from the table and you had to have really good manners.

Ted Frost

Schooldays at Ryecroft Infants and Rosehill

I was in the scholarship class at Rosehill; that was Miss Holroyd's class. I remember taking the County Scholarship [the equivalent of the 11 Plus]. I had to write an essay about my favourite lesson and I wrote about needlework, even though I hated it in school. When I told my mother I had written about needlework she couldn't believe it and said, 'You've failed then.' I had written that my very favourite part of the lesson was when the teacher

went out of the room and we could all have a good natter. When we heard the sound of approaching footsteps we all scuttled back to our places. My mother said, 'Do you realise you will get that teacher the sack?' After that I spent weeks worrying that that was what would happen.

After that I got whooping cough rather badly and had to be isolated for weeks. A letter arrived from school while I was absent and my mother thought it would be about my absence and said she would refer them to Dr Lister. Then she opened the envelope and it said that your daughter has

Mary Ferns in her Mexborough Secondary School uniform. Notice the short socks!

passed the County Scholarship. She couldn't believe it. So I moved on to Mexborough Secondary School in 1935. At that time far more children from Rawmarsh went on to Mexborough rather than Wath. I caught the trackless to Mexborough and you had to wear your uniform perfectly on the trackless or you would get into trouble. I was told off there because I wanted to wear short white socks, but the uniform was long white socks. Needless to say I had to change! Overall though I thought it was an excellent school, I loved it there. I don't think a bit of discipline when you are young does you any harm.

Mary Ferns

Russell's Commercial School

I went to Ryecroft Infants and then on to Rosehill. Very few passed the 11 Plus and I didn't. Some of my friends still went to Wath Grammar School because their parents paid for them. Although my dad was brilliant at maths he hadn't gone to the grammar school because they were too poor and they couldn't afford the uniform and all the rest.

He went into the pits the day he was fourteen. I went to the Haugh Road School for a year and a half and then my dad paid for me to go to Russell's Commercial School at Mexborough. As we were still of school age we had to do all the normal school lessons as well as shorthand, typing and book-keeping.

Joyce Bray

A young Joyce Bray at Wheatcroft Road.

The smell of wet rubber macs

I didn't pass the 11 Plus, but I got into Mexborough through their entrance exam. It was a secondary school when I first went and then it changed to a grammar school. This was near the end of the war. I used to get the trolleybus from Rosehill Park to Mexborough and the bus was full with a large number of children from Rawmarsh going to Wath or Mexborough schools. We used to work from nine to half-past three. If you arrived late for school you had to go in through the front door and you would have to explain yourself. I think I was only late once. I felt really funny and I said to my friend, 'I'm going to have to get off the bus and walk because of the smell of all the wet rubber macs.'

The winter of 1947 was really bad, but as far as I can remember we only had one day off school. On that day the trolleybus wires were all frozen up. When it started thawing we didn't realise and started walking to Swinton to catch the bus at the railway station. At the bridge at the end of Mexborough the ground was absolutely sodden and my shoes got soaked. Them with Wellingtons were all right, but we couldn't get any for love nor money even though we had the coupons; there were none in the shops. The buses were turning round at Swinton station because it was flooded under the bridge.

Freda Stacey

A Swinton and Mexborough trolleybus on which Freda Stacey found the smell of wet rubber macs overpowering.

11 Plus problems

I started at Ashwood Road School when I was three and the headmaster then was Mr Firth. Other teachers I had there were Mr Pengelly (he was bald and used to cane you), Miss Walker, Mr Wilcocks and Miss Downing. I thought I got a really good education there. I didn't pass the 11 Plus, but we weren't prepared for it at all we just went into the hall one day and did the exam. I know I spent too long on the questions and didn't finish. I went on to Haugh Road and I remember there was a girl called Esme Hannah and she came to school for a time because her father was serving as a sergeant up at the POW camp on Greasbrough Tops.

Danny Larder

Danny Larder on a trip out with other children. His grandma Lottie Wassell was in charge.

Walking on the hedges

I was born in Kilnhurst Road and went to South Street School and then on to Rosehill Junior. In 1947 I moved to Mexborough Secondary, which was renamed Mexborough Grammar in 1948. We were encouraged to apply to Mexborough from Rosehill if the 11 Plus was passed, but you could choose between Mexborough and Wath. The headmaster at Rosehill when I was there was Mr Bedford. My last year at Rosehill was the year of the bad winter in 1947 and I can remember walking along the top of the hedge to get from home to school because the snow was so deep on the footpath. The Italian prisoners-of-war had cleared the road and put all the snow where the footpath was. The snow there was level with the top of the hedges.

Frank Horner

Come-uppance

I started school around 1951 at St Joseph's, Green Lane, and I started early. I'll never forget the day I started. We used to have to walk up Barber's Avenue and down Green Lane to take my sister Lorraine to school. I can remember skipping up to school and teasing my sister on the way saying, 'You're going to school and I'm going shopping.' At the school the headmistress, Miss Addiss, said to my mum that there was a spare place in school and that she could leave Yvonne there and then. It certainly cheered up my sister!

Miss Addiss was a lovely headmistress and she lived at the bottom of Barber's Avenue. Other teachers there were Mary Moloney, Delia Langdon and Mrs Heaney. They were nice teachers, but very strict. I think there were four classes in the school at that time. The classrooms were separated by partitions that could be pushed aside to make a hall and that's where Mass was at first. The church was built while I was at school and that's when they built the grotto; that is very, very special. We used to have a sleep when I first went to school; we used fold-up beds and blankets. In the best weather in summer we could go to sleep outside in the fresh air. I didn't go to sleep very often as I went to bed at 7 p.m. in winter and 7.30 p.m. in summer. One of the boys at school was Anthony Turner, he lived opposite the tram sheds and his father was Bobby Turner, a policeman. He could give you a clip round the ear if he saw you doing something wrong on the street.

Yvonne Harrison

Football with Alick Jeffrey

I played football for the school team at Haugh Road all the time from 1949 till I left in 1953. We never lost a match in all that time. I played for Rotherham Boys as well; we played at Millmoor and at Rawmarsh Welfare a lot. Alick Jeffrey played for us at Haugh Road and Rotherham Boys before going on to Doncaster Rovers and the Young England team. Alick and I were inside forwards in the Rotherham Boys team and then there was Pete Vernon as well. There were quite a few from Rotherham Grammar in the team at that time. Rotherham Boys team had three internationals in it then. Ironically we ended up without a goalkeeper because the goalie we had began playing for Swinton Welfare and you weren't allowed to play for the boys team if you were in a senior team. Later on Alick was the best man at my wedding.

Danny Larder

The all-conquering Haugh Road football team with Danny Larder seated centre, Alick Jeffrey standing third from the left and their teacher Mr Cartwright.

Lots of singing

I went to school at St Joseph's and I started in 1958. The headmistress was Miss Addiss and she seemed very strict. It was very old-fashioned Catholic but some of the people there were kind. There was a bit too much hell-fire and damnation but it was quite a close community and what I really liked was we did a lot of singing. I did become an altar boy eventually and the priests I can remember from then were Father Woodhouse and Father Killeen. Later I went on to the De La Salle Grammar School in Sheffield.

Ray Hearne

Snow days

It was lovely when it snowed, but you still had to go to school. Living in Rawmarsh, we had to walk to Pope Pius in Wath. When I first started it was tracklesses we used, but they might not run in snow. The snow was really deep sometimes and we were wet by the time we got to school. It was much better walking back at the end of school because we were going home. At least we had a cloakroom to hang up our coats when we got to school and had a chance to dry. When we went sledging we went down Roundwood, on the fields there. We used to get wet through but you didn't feel it. We would get hot aches in our fingers. When we went home we often had toast heated up in front of the fire. We played cricket and rounders at Roundwood too.

Yvonne Harrison

Secondary school at Mexborough

I was one of six pupils from Netherfield Lane who passed the County Minor Scholarship – five of us attended Mexborough Secondary School. I recall the apprehension I felt at first, facing a journey of thirty minutes by trackless, eating school dinners and finding my way around. I quickly adapted to my new situation and the feeling that I was a small pebble on a vast beach soon receded. I joined the choir and in the fifth form was cajoled into playing in the hockey team.

When war came, circumstances changed. Eligible male members of staff were called up to active service and were replaced by elderly teachers who came out of retirement. Extra-curricular activities were curtailed because of the blackout but we still managed to enjoy the life.

Marian Overland at
Netherfield Lane Infant
School.

One memory I shall always have occurred when there was a heavy fall of snow during
the day. Though we were dismissed early, the tracklesses were called off the road. It seemed
we were stranded. We set out to walk home in the cold and slushy blackness. Warren Vale
has never seemed so long. My mum was concerned and set out with my brother to look
for me. What a relief when we met at the end of Netherfield Lane!

Marian Overland

Johnny Teal tore it up

I started school at the infant school in Dale Road. Johnny Cater was the first headmaster there. Then I went on to the other Dale Road School and there was a teacher there called Johnny Teal, who lived in Stocks Lane. There were about forty in each class there. I thought the teachers were good. I was there when Edward VIII abdicated and there was a picture of him up on the wall at school. When he abdicated Johnny Teal took down the picture and tore it up. I can remember that gas masks and the cardboard boxes to keep them in were sent to school six months before the war started.

I was eleven when war was declared. I was meant to start at Haugh Road School but we were six weeks late starting because they had to build air-raid shelters in the playground there. When I went there all the younger men teachers were in the army so we had all women teachers. The headmaster was 'Pa' White; he had been my dad's captain in the Yorks and Lancs during the First World War. Mr White's wife came in to teach us art and she was brilliant. We had Mrs Pettigrew for gym then. I left school at fourteen and went to Rotherham Tech for two years on a building course. Most of my mates from school either went into the steelworks or into the pits. Later I got a job working at Cooper's at Greasbrough as a bound apprentice. You served a seven-year apprenticeship then.

Albert Evans

Albert Evans, showing off an impressive pair of knees.

three

GROWING UP

Dale Road prims

We all went to Dale Road Primitive Methodist Chapel, known as the 'Prims', where we had many happy times. In 1907, when we first joined, it was a very thriving place. On Sunday evening if you weren't in church by 5.30 p.m. you couldn't get a seat. Some of the preachers we had in those days were real ranters. After chapel every Sunday night during the light nights we went out to give outdoor services. We used to visit the different yards and usually the preacher went with us. I remember one Sunday night when a very funny thing happened. We had a Missioner who was full of praise of the Lord. We went to the Pump Yard that night and he wanted a chair to stand on so everybody could see him. They all kept pigs in that yard, so someone put a board across the top of a swill tub for him to stand on. He announced the first hymn which was 'Fixed on this ground will I remain, till earth's foundations melt away' and he was so enthusiastic about it that he jumped about to show his feelings and the board came off the swill tub and he fell into the swill! It was very funny and the open-air service ended in lots of laughter. He was taken to one of the houses to get cleaned up and he had to be fitted out in spare clothes to get him home as he lived in Sheffield.

We had a very good Sunday school, with a cricket eleven and a football team – all grand young men who would do anything for anybody. Once a month there was a Saturday night social evening and you only had to let it be known to the surrounding houses in Chapel Street and the food that turned up was marvellous; meat pies, fruit pies, cakes, bread, scones, in fact everything you could mention. Afterwards everything was cleared up and made ready for Sunday school next day.

We had something going on every night of the week. On Wednesdays we had the Band of Hope. Our leader was a very notable character whose name was Mr George Haigh. He was very much against drinking, and we, as children, were urged to sign the pledge and stick to it. We all had a good laugh at him, though I don't think that he realised why we used to laugh so much. We always closed the meeting with the hymn 'My Drink is Water Bright'. Mr Haigh was so enthusiastic about it that he would shout, 'And put some spirit in it!' We all thought this was very funny and I'm sure he didn't realise what he was saying.

Elsie Beaumont

At the parish church

I went to the parish church and to Sunday school there when I was young. Later I belonged to the Girls' Friendly Society and we used to meet in the Church Room. We took part in competitions for dancing and other performances. I've got a photo of us when we did a skating dance to represent the four seasons of the year. I was representing winter and my cousin Elsie Painter was my partner.

We went on a trip to London once with the society and it was led by Miss Bielby, who was a teacher at Dale Road. We met Canon Scovell and his wife in London and they took us around and showed us all the sights.

Edith Schofield

The Friendly Society's cast for the *Four Seasons* performance around 1920, with Edith Schofield standing on the extreme left.

The Christ Church First XI in 1910. They played football to a very high standard at that time.

A Bradbury in your pocket

I was brought up in Victoria Road and part of the area nearby in Infirmary Road was called Casey Court. It was like a joke name from one of the comics at the time. I remember going in the tin chapel on Infirmary Road and Mr Barker, who took the service there, said, 'Children, there are two things in life that matter; one is the love of Jesus in your heart and the other is a "Bradbury" in your pocket.' [A 'Bradbury' was a pound note in the 1920s and '30s signed by a cashier called Bradbury.] Christ Church used to play football beyond Victoria Road and my dad was on the committee. We often used to go away with the team on Smart's coaches. They played in the Sheffield League with Rawmarsh Athletic and Greasbrough. I first learned to drink coffee there when I used to take the drinks out to the players at half time. Parkgate Welfare played further up the hill on Hospital Fields.

Henry Lowry

Our own entertainment

I started life in Dale Road, opposite the old school and then we moved into a Fitzwilliam cottage on High Street. It was in a yard near the council yard. The cottages there were very old, with thick walls and deep windows. They had no damp-course or anything like that. We moved because we needed extra bedrooms and it had three.

My father, John Hill, was a pipe fitter at Stubbin pit, before that he had worked at Oxley's steelworks. Ernest Jackson, from the council, always used to come and get him when something went wrong with the urinal that was close by on the High Street. It was always leaking and causing trouble. My mother was Dorothy Ward, who was linked with the fruit shop.

When I was young and still living on Dale Road I can remember Saturday afternoons with hundreds of men coming down Peashill Street to Hill Sixty where the football team played. We used to make our own entertainment. At Ward's fruit and vegetable shop onions and oranges came in their own boxes tied together with rope and we used to use it to make skipping ropes. Nothing was ever wasted then. We used to go down Titanic Steps and a bit further on when there were no houses there. We used to collect clay there and mould it into snobs; if you bought them they were all coloured, but ours were just clay coloured.

A group of pupils from Rosehill School on a trip to Hoober Stand. Among the girls are Marjorie Oxer (*née* Hill), Enid Boulton, Ethel Badger and Edna Scott.

Rawmarsh High Street with Ward's greengrocers on the left, where Marjorie Oxer collected rope to use for skipping.

Marjorie Oxer

Floods in Parkgate

I can remember some bad floods when I was young, it must have been about 1931. All the houses at Stone Row in Parkgate were flooded and you had to get off the bus at one side of the flood and get round to the other side to catch another bus into town. You could buy tickets then for a shilling that did you for twelve rides. We didn't often go into Rotherham, although the first film I saw was in the Essoldo in Doncaster Gate, Rotherham, with Al Jolson in it. We did most of our shopping in Parkgate although at Christmas time we went up to Sheffield to look at the shops like Walsh's and Schofield's.

Muriel Sykes

My father's funeral

I can remember one of the blast furnaces in Aldwarke Road being built. My father used to work sometimes on the other side of a high brick wall near the furnaces and my mother would give me sandwiches to take for him and he would lean down over the wall and collect them. When my father died they closed the works gates on both sides of

Rotherham Road and brought an engine to each side to stand by the gates as his funeral went past. They took him to Rotherham to be cremated. Living next to Christ Church, I remember the funerals very well, with the glass-sided hearse and the black horses wearing plumes pulling it. The chief mourners had to wear black and even had to borrow black clothes from neighbours if they had none suitable themselves.

Nellie Schofield

The first films

I remember when films first came to Rawmarsh. I can't recall who brought them but for two weeks all the children were allowed in free to see them. They were very sad pictures and made us all cry. During the interval a young man called Colty Acom came on and did a bit of clowning and sang a song which began 'Ten a penny and they're all cracked'; I can't remember the rest of it. Acom's had a grocer's shop opposite Stocks Lane. At that time, I think it would be about 1910, there was a gas lamp in the middle of the road at the top of Stocks Lane which was removed when they put the tram lines in.

Elsie Beaumont

Visit to the war cemeteries

My dad worked at Aldwarke pit, which was a John Brown's pit, and he used to come up to Warren House on Saturdays to pay the miners, as he was a cashier. I used to go with him when he went to Warren House. I can remember taking a little beaker with me for a drink of tea. My dad used to play a lot of cricket. Mother was a teacher at Rosehill but she stopped working as soon as she got married. You didn't carry on working after you married unless you were widowed. Really unusually, my dad took my mother to Belgium in 1926 to see the war cemeteries. He'd been in the First World War but he'd been invalided out. They sailed from Hull to Zeebrugge.

Freda Stacey

Visiting the Crystal Palace

I can remember going on trips with the Sons of Temperance when I was young. We went to places like Cleethorpes. The Sons of Temperance were based at the Methodist church.

Leonard and Muriel Sykes, who were married on Christmas Day 1939.

on High Street. We used to have a meeting once a fortnight and also on a Saturday night. We never took much notice of how long the trips took, but I suppose it was about two hours with a stop on the way. I went to the Crystal Palace in London as well. There were six of us from the Sons of Temperance. We travelled by train at midnight, so it was a long journey. The Crystal Palace was packed but we didn't go inside, we just walked round outside. We also used to walk into Rotherham to catch the train to Blackpool. It cost 2*s* 6*d* for an evening trip to Blackpool. This was well before the Second World War.

Muriel Sykes

Going on holiday

When we went away on holiday after the war you had to send your luggage on before you, usually on the Wednesday before the Saturday you got the train. It was the same when you came back. It was a real problem when you didn't have many clothes. You had to make

Margaret Horner, Joyce and Cyril Bray can all be seen on the left of this photograph, appearing in a play at Ryecroft Methodist Church.

sure you got it to and from the railway station. You had to take your tinned food with you too. We used to get the train at Parkgate for Scarborough, changing at York. We went in the pit holiday weeks, so you met people from Rawmarsh and Parkgate in Scarborough. The main places for holidays were Scarborough, Bridlington or Skegness. The first time I went to London I went with Cyril on the midnight train. It got in at about five o'clock. We went for breakfast at Lyons Corner House.

Joyce Bray

Whit Parades

We used to have big processions at Whitsuntide. At first we used to have all the Sunday Schools, all behind their own banner, and we paraded up to Rosehill Park and sang hymns there around the bandstand and led by the Salvation Army Band. Later they had a more decorated procession with tableaux on the back of lorries. Rawmarsh Congregational

Nellie Schofield can be found in this Whit Parade of 1923 standing with her chapel's maypole.

One of the Whit Parade tableaux that were an important part of the celebrations in Rawmarsh.

Chapel always used to excel in the competitions. We used to carry a decorated maypole and every year it was re-trimmed. The strings were decorated with coloured paper and twelve girls each held a string. We also wore crepe-paper bonnets. My mother made those bonnets for several years. We used to walk from Lloyd Street and join the others at the bottom of the hill in Greasbrough Road. After the singing in the park we had our teas there. Each Sunday school had a little bit of the park allocated to them and Lakes, the milk people, used to lend us their lorry and the primary children rode in it. They used to bring the lorry back to the chapel and tea was made before it was taken back up to the park. I can't remember it ever raining on those Whit Mondays. We used to practise singing the hymns for weeks before the procession.

Nellie Schofield

Clothes for the 'Pop' Shop

After the night-soil men had cleared out the middens at my grandparents' house in Dale Street, the next morning it would all be done with fresh white lime. I cringe with horror now when I think what all the little girls used to do. We used to get the net curtains

Charlotte Clarkson, Noreen Brown's grandmother, sits in this family group with her sister Mary. She lived in Dale Street and made regular use of the local pawnbroker's.

and play pretend weddings and throw the lime over each other. I can remember that my grandma had a great big bed of mint outside in the back and we always used to visit for Sunday tea. I always used to think that they had lamb for dinner because of the smell of mint, but when I said this to mother she said no, everyone grew mint next to their outside toilet to hide the smell!

My grandma was Charlotte Clarkson (*née* Simmons) and my mother could remember the old lady who used to visit her on Monday mornings with a great big shawl to collect all the clothes for the 'Pop' Shop. She hid them under the shawl so you weren't seen

A wedding party at the Rumpelstiltskin pub on Church Street, *c.* 1900. The wedding was between Fred Nix and Jessie Tate. The pub does not seem to have been in existence for long.

'popping' your clothes. They would get them out again when my grandad got paid at the weekend. They would get them out, wear their Sunday clothes and then get them taken back on Monday morning. My grandma gave the old lady a shilling for doing it. My mother, as a child, used to get a new pair of plimsolls every Saturday morning for a shilling and they would just last a week. She never had actual shoes.

Noreen Brown

Life in Low End

Parkgate was a wonderful playground for a young lad. There were a couple of 'bucket heaps' on some waste ground. The heaps were conical-shaped spoil hills from some previous workings which had been abandoned. The two hills were quite close together so the top was like a two-humped camel. You could run down one, gather speed and the momentum would take you up the other one. This was my favourite place for playing.

A crowd of veritable 'urchins' standing across Stanley Street in the Low End of Parkgate and celebrating the end of the First World War.

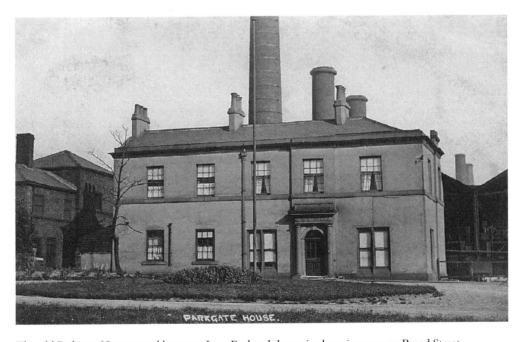

The old Parkgate House stood between Low End and the main shopping area on Broad Street.

Bill Whitehouse, my stepfather, worked at Aldwarke Main. Occasionally I had to accompany him to work, collect his wages and bring them home – with great warnings to look after them. To get to Aldwarke Main we had to walk on Collier's Walk, which ran along the side of the LMS railway line and emerged down at Aldwarke, just opposite the actual colliery. Collier's Walk became a favourite of mine because between the walk and the railway bank puddles of water gathered and gradually formed pools which stayed there all the year round. Football was a popular pastime which we could play on a bit of wasteland at the back of the Sunday school [Ebenezer Chapel]. I was always pleased when Sunday school was over; I would dash home and change into my football togs. I remember Kenny Lamb, Sam and Frank Whitehouse were some of the regular players.

Les Coe

Water like jelly

At home the water was heated up in the set-pot, the copper, and put in an iron bath to do the washing. Once all the washing was finished all of us children would get in the bath one at a time for our weekly bath. By the time the last one went in, the water was thick; you could pick it up like a jelly! Normally the bath was hung on a nail in the back yard. We had a stone sink and one cold tap on the sink. We had a water toilet across the yard, although before I was born it was an ash midden. Every winter everything froze up. The winters were much worse then.

Albert Evans

An ash midden was once a familiar sight for the people of Rawmarsh and Parkgate.

In the oven

We used to keep hens outside our house and quite often they used to escape into Lilley's Yard. We had a little black hen that was one of our best layers and it always used to 'lay away' under the gooseberries. We loved the black hen because it was quite tame really. 'Blacky' used to go missing and a couple of times I had to go and ask for it back from Mrs Lilley as it had gone through the hedge. Then one day Blacky disappeared again and my mother sent me round to ask Mrs Lilley if she had seen her. Rather brusquely she said she had and told me to come in. She pointed to the oven and said 'There she is!' I was absolutely heart-broken, I came back home in floods of tears. My mother was livid about it.

We also used to have some ducks and there was a pig in a sty next to the garage. I can remember the pig always being covered in mud. I thought it was horrible. Next to the pig-sty was the midden. When I was little my mum said the night-soil men would be coming to empty the midden. All our rubbish went on the midden. One day mum said we were getting something new, it was called a dustbin. From then on we stopped using the midden.

Mary Ferns

A wedding group of the Lilley family shown in Hill's Yard on Rawmarsh High Street around 1908.

Mary Ferns as a youngster.

Picking blackberries

We used to like walking down to Kilnhurst because there were lots of lovely meadows to walk through with wild flowers; 'Concrete Canyon' wasn't there at that time. We went down there at the end of the summer to pick blackberries to put in fruit pies. We used to go across the river on a ferry and get the blackberries from the woods nearby. We put the blackberries in basins to bring them home. We would go to the park sometimes, with a bottle of water and a jam sandwich, and stop there for most of the day. We went up without any adults; you could just wander around then.

Dad was a keen cricket umpire and we often went to watch Rawmarsh Cricket Club play. He was also a fanatical Rotherham United fan. After the war there were so many people going into Rotherham on a Saturday afternoon for the match that you couldn't get on a bus. People from Parkgate used to come up to Ryecroft to the terminus so they could get on a bus to Rotherham. It was no good waiting in Parkgate for a bus to Rotherham, they all went through full.

Joyce Bray

Joyce Bray's walks to Kilnhurst sometimes included a return via Aldwarke Lock, shown here being used by two barges.

Joyce Bray often went to cricket matches with her dad. Here the Rawmarsh Welfare team are led out for Alf Goulden's Benefit Match.

Games round the gas lamp

For recreation my dad and Uncle Harold would take my mum's clothes line when she wasn't looking, go to the front onto the spare bit of land and turn the rope with great big arm sweeps for us all to skip. There would be ten or twelve of us skipping at the same time.

My cousin Keith and I would go together down Roundwood fields and cross the railway lines at the crossing. After crossing the LMS line we would walk a little way and stand on a bridge over the LNER line and wait for the *Flying Scotsman* to come through. This was a wonderful green train. When it passed under the bridge the smoke was so dense we couldn't see a thing, but we were always very excited when we heard the train coming. Also, we would take a picnic to Rosehill Park and eat it as soon as we got there! I played mostly with boys because all my cousins on my mother's side were boys. There were some girls at the bottom of Green Lane and we played snobs, marbles, ball and tiggy round the gas lamp. The lamp-lighter, Mr Guy, used to come round every night on his old

Hercules bike with a very long pole and light the gas lamp. Not during the war years of course. He used to ride his bike with one hand and carry his great long pole with the other. Absolutely amazing!

Traffic was very light. A horse and dray would come around with fruit and veg, or just veg if there was no fruit. A coal lorry would come around delivering free coal to all the miners. Mrs Clegg from our local farm came round every day, delivering milk in her pony and trap. She carried a churn of milk and a smaller churn to our back door, measured the milk with a gill measuring jug and then poured it into our jug.

Joan Gillions

Joan Gillion's father, Arthur Mitchell, got a job initially as the flour-boy at Foxton's on Barber's Avenue. He is pictured here in his working clothes.

Joan Gillions (*née* Mitchell) playing in the garden of 129 Green Lane with Raymond, Eric and Jack.

An extended family group enjoying a day out in Rosehill Park. Joan Gillions is one of the group.

In the Isolation Hospital

I spent about nine or ten weeks in the Isolation Hospital at Rosehill when I was about eight or nine. I had scarlet fever and then, when I was getting better, I caught chickenpox and had to stay in for an extra two weeks. My mum and dad could only speak to me through the glass of the window and the doctor and nurses were always gowned-up and masked. All I wore was a pair of blue shorts and they scratched bad – they were rough!

Ray Hague

Snided with black clocks

My family were the Bantons and they were very keen fishermen and cyclists. My mother's mother lived on Victoria Road and that's where I was born. Every Saturday morning me and my sister had to go down to Kilnhurst Co-op with my mother's and grand-mother's orders and bring back their rations (this was during the war). We had to walk it over the fields and when we got back, one of us had to rubbing stone the steps and window ledges while the other did the kitchen floor which was made of red tiles. My grandmother used to make this paste with flour to use on the floor, but all the houses were snided with black clocks and they used to come out at night to feast on the floor.

Joyce Hawley

The fields at Mangham

In the summertime we used to cycle to Roche Abbey. I had a really old black bicycle with a basket on the front. I used to take a bottle of water, dripping sandwiches and lettuce sandwiches. We had an abundance of lettuce because my mum used to grow it. When we came down to Aldwarke we had to pay a tiny lady a toll to get through the toll gates. This was just me and my friends. We used to cycle down Mangham and there was a place down there where you could swim. We also went to Langold Lake to swim there. We used to visit Joan Ratcliffe at Mangham and Lorraine and I played with Joan's daughter Mary in the fields around there.

Yvonne Harrison

Yvonne Harrison plays with her sister Lorraine and Mary Ratcliffe in the fields at Mangham.

Four times to chapel

My Bailey grandparents lived down Kilnhurst Road and ran a shop from the house. My parents and uncle went to the old Ryecroft chapel and so did I. The ministers I can remember from then were Revd Hull and Revd Hutchinson. I used to go to the chapel four times on a Sunday; first for Sunday school and then the morning service, followed by another Sunday school in the afternoon and then the evening service. We weren't really allowed to do anything else on Sundays. You couldn't play with a ball nor on the swings in the park, although you could go for a walk there. You couldn't buy anything either on a Sunday nor have anything bought for you unless you were on holiday. One of my relatives used to want to buy me an ice cream at Sunday teatime, but I had to say no. On Sunday evenings in summer we used to go to Rosehill Park to listen to the band; it was usually the Rawmarsh Prize Band or a colliery band. There used to be a lot of people doing the same. We sometimes carried on to walk through Birchwood.

Margaret Horner

A crowd in Rosehill Park sitting around the bandstand.

King Kong is coming!

When I was about five or six years old there was a film around called *King Kong*. One day in the holidays I heard someone say they had seen King Kong coming up Warren Vale. I ran up Dale Road and charged into the house and rushed upstairs. My mother wondered what on earth was happening, but I was absolutely terrified.

Ron Liversidge

Betting on the Whit Parade

I started school at Ryecroft Infant and then went on to Rosehill. When I started singing with the Rawmarsh Choral Society many years later I found out they rehearsed in Ryecroft Infant School, so I went back to my first school! We used to go to the Congregational Chapel on the corner of Stocks Lane. There was a service in the morning and the evening on Sundays and I went to the Sunday school. We also went to the Sisterhood on Mondays. We always used to really look forward to the Sunday school outing to Bridlington. It was always in June. Miss Stones, a teacher, used to collect our pennies each week and we always

Sunday school outings to Bridlington were always looked forward to by Joan Pearce, especially the boat rides.

Joan Pearce as the Cong's 1937 May Queen with two attendants.

The members of the Rawmarsh Congregational Church were a very active part of the local community. Here they can be seen at a bazaar in 1951.

went by coach. We always stopped at Holme-on-Spalding-Moor and always had a bag of Smith's crisps, with the salt in the blue twist of paper. Every year my Uncle John took us for a ride on the *Boy's Own* boat when we got to Bridlington. On the way home Miss Stones would give us each a stick of rock.

Another big event each year was the Whit procession. We used to spend ages decorating our maypole at the Congregational Chapel and practising the hymns. We used to join the procession on Rawmarsh Hill and then parade along to Rosehill Park. We used to do really well in the competitions and you could hear the men betting each other who was going to win.

Joan Pearce

Doncaster Race Week

Doncaster Race Week was a big event locally. People used to go to the races in a charabanc that belonged to Matt Hawley from Dale Road (he had a greengrocer's shop there). My mum used to go with my dad for a day, even though she didn't bet. On the day they went

I had to go to my Grandma Pursglove's house for dinner from school and then back there after school. When the charabanc came back up Kilnhurst hill it used to stop and all the kids would surround it and shout 'Throw us your winnings' and they used to throw out butterscotch for them all. My mother was always obsessed with the beautiful silks the jockeys wore.

Edna Pease

The penny rush

On a Friday night I got bathed at John Turner's house because they had hot water and we didn't. We lived in the same yard in New Street. His mother and my mother used to take us to the first house at the Regal. We also went to Robbie's, often in a big group,

seven or eight of us. Robbie's was a legend. There was a little toffee shop in the corner and it opened at half time between the little pictures and the big pictures, when the news was on. You always knew the big pictures were about to start because you could hear the breaking toffee! You charged down to get in the queue and took your piece of newspaper to put your toffee in. You got newsprint all over your toffee! We weren't rich enough to go upstairs.

The 'penny rush' started at about half past four on a Wednesday for all the kids. You had to sit downstairs on the benches at the front; all the red velvet seats at the back were off limits and covered with white sheets. We were all packed onto the benches and if you didn't move up you'd be

The Methodist church on High Street that was converted into Robbie's picture house, site of the 'penny rush'.

brayed by Mrs Robinson with a roll of wallpaper. The floor was made of wood and the kids used to roll glass bottles down to the front to make a noise. They used to bang up against the stage at the front. Then Robbie would come in to investigate; 'You young devils,' he would shout.

I can remember going to see *Psycho* when I was courting and we went upstairs in the 'love seats'. These were double seats at the back. Everyone would be fighting to get them. All the seats upstairs were the same price; I think they were about a shilling. At the end, old man Robbie, who looked like Wild Bill Hickok with his long flowing white hair and Stetson hat, would stand near the door with a cigar and say, 'Goodnight. Mind the mat.' Robbie would announce the films when it wasn't the penny rush, 'Ladies and gentlemen we have a bumper programme for you this evening. We have Lauren Bacall and Humphrey Bogart.' One of the projectionists was a lad called Tommy Foster. He went on to be a projectionist at the Regal.

Ron Liversidge

Biking to Clumber

When we were young we used to cycle a lot. We used to go to places like Clumber Park or Edwinstowe and we would bike it all the way. When we set off we always used to call at a little grocer's shop opposite the Green Lane Tavern which had a chewing gum machine. We used to get two chewing gums for a ha'penny. We used to have that chewing gum all the way to Edwinstowe and all the way back! When we did we had to pay a penny to take each of our bikes through the Aldwarke toll gate. I didn't like walking over the river down there at Aldwarke because you could see the water through the gaps in the wooden bridge. My mum and dad had a tandem with a sidecar on it! Me and Cliff borrowed it once when we were courting; we went to Denaby.

Joyce Hawley

Bonfire night

On 5 November we used to have a bonfire in the big field over the dyke from Church Street. We used to have some roast taters and a few fireworks. We collected sleepers, trees, boxes and cardboard for the fire. The family used to get together at the bonfire. The 4 November was Mischievous Night. We used to make 'window tappers' with a safety pin, a bit of cotton or string and with a button or a piece of wood. It would keep tapping the window when you pulled the string. We used to tie up the door handles as well. It was

A view of Top Pottery Street, one of the homes of Rawmarsh's little gangs.

only in our street and they all knew who was doing it. One year we dressed up one of the smallest kids as a 'guy' in a barrow. He was dressed up in rags and we painted his face. We nearly got rumbled when one bloke in Westfield Road said to bring him in so he could have a good look. He had to sit very still! There were little gangs from each street like Netherfield Lane, Lloyd Street and Pottery Street, but there was never any real trouble, it was handbags at dawn stuff.

Ray Hague

Collecting for the nurses

I used to go round the houses with my mother every week and collect for the district nurses. The nurses had a house on the corner of Vesey Street. When we collected this money we used to take it in there. They were mainly midwives there. Nurse Wheldon was the nurse in charge. We never went in the house, we just went to the door to hand in the money.

Sheila Skeldon

A group of the Queen's nurses from the corner of Vesey Street that Sheila Skeldon collected money for.

'Ladding it'

We used to walk along from the baths hall all the way nearly into Haugh on a Sunday night. People used to call this the 'monkey run'. We were about fifteen or sixteen, you know when we were 'ladding it'. People who lived on there used to complain about all the young people hanging around. This was in the winter; in the summer we walked round the gardens in the park. There used to be a band playing in the park every Sunday. It used to be packed watching the band and it was all free. Miss Ackroyd used to run the Rawmarsh Prize Band.

Muriel Sykes

Haugh Road about 1935, the site of the 'monkey run' as described by Muriel Sykes.

A school group, including Walker Scales, visiting Hoober Stand. Many children went on their own expeditions there in the summer holidays.

Making some pocket money

In the summer holidays we used to make a bit of money by taking Pickering's barrow down to Aldwarke pit to collect wood. The barrow wheels came from old mangles! We clubbed together and paid a tanner for this wood and then chopped it into sticks to sell to people. We used to put the sticks in buckets to be sold for people's fires at a penny a bucket. We arranged the sticks so as few as possible were used to fill the bucket, but most people saw through that. We also went off on whole day expeditions to places like Hoober Stand and Listerdale Woods. We'd take our sandwiches and a water bottle. We also started collecting wood in the holidays to use on Bonfire Night. Later on, in October, we used to do potato picking, especially at Norman Hobson's farm at Haugh. They used to go round hawking potatoes. Mrs Hobson would come round with the sixpenny card and drop in a sack of potatoes. There were also carts came round hawking rabbits, especially on Saturday nights about seven or eight o'clock. They were from Rotherham and owned by Sammy Morton.

John Turner

Scared in the churchyard

When we went to the 'penny rush' at Robbie's we would set out from Church Street across the churchyard. When it was getting dark, in autumn and winter time, about eight of the lads used to get in amongst the gravestones and scare us by jumping up. We used to run! There was only one gas lamp on the left and one where you turned the corner,

Edna Vaughan is pictured here in the middle of a group of girls at Ashwood Road School. Her experiment with hair styling was not completely successful!

but when it was windy the lamps would go out. I know who scared us because my future husband was one of them!

We used to save our pennies when we could. I used to go up Aldwarke Road from Ashwood Road School to a shop called Lee's that sold lovely pottery and I used to put down so much each week to buy a present for my mother for Christmas. I got a penny for going to the fish shop and perhaps a ha'penny for collecting jam jars and taking them back to the shop. I bought two vases and they were about a shilling a piece.

That's me in the middle at the front of the school photo. This is at Ashwood Road School about 1924. My friend has lovely curly hair because she put rags in it at night. Before the photo I asked my mum to put rags in mine. She said it wouldn't work but I insisted. The following day I couldn't even get a comb through it!

Edna Vaughan

Whisky in the tea

At Christmas we used to get an orange, an apple and one or two new pennies and then there was your main present and a box of chocolates that cost sixpence ha'penny. You didn't get overloaded with presents like nowadays. We always had a piece of pork for dinner on Christmas Day and then all the family came for tea; meat, salad, trifle and cake. We didn't have much money, but we always put on a good spread. My father used to get a bottle of Black and White Horse Whisky and at the end of the meal he went round the table and put a drop in everyone's tea. You probably got a bottle of whisky then for about half a crown.

On New Year's Eve and New Year's Day we used to go round the houses on the lower part of Kilnhurst Road performing the Derby Tup. It was a bit like a Mummer's play. My uncle, Arthur Pursglove, (who worked on the railway at Kilnhurst) and my cousin, Alan Pursglove, used to perform. I think one of the men dressed up in women's clothes. I wasn't in the play, I just stood in the background. Arthur and Alan had to sing some sort of a ditty.

Edna Pease

Is there a Mary Pearson here?

I never used to go to Robbie's. My mother wouldn't let me go. One day my Aunt Cathy was looking after me and I asked her if I could go to the pictures with some friends. She agreed, so I was really excited. I sat right at the front and I can remember being a bit worried about all these camels walking across the screen so close. They seemed to be right on top of me. I didn't seem to be there long before the picture stopped and Mr Robinson got up on the stage and said 'Is there a Mary Pearson here? Will she come immediately, her mother wants her.' You can imagine how embarrassed I was. So I went home and she was livid. She said, 'You must never ever go to the pictures; it's going to the devil.' That was all my experience of the pictures.

Mary Ferns

The pig killer

I was born at No. 8 Church Street, ninety years ago this year. It was lovely there when we were kiddies because we had all the fields to play in. It was a great place to go sledging in winter. The road was surfaced at the top, but not at the bottom. There was a row of houses at the top of the road and then a big bit of land, then there were two houses and then another row of houses. The unmade road at the bottom, where Granny Vaughan lived, had pigeon lofts next to it. Everybody had hens and the Brothertons, nearly next door, had pigs. A man used to come to kill the pigs. Mum used to say, 'They're killing the pigs today.' I used to go on the stairs and cover my ears and face with a towel so I couldn't hear or see anything. I used to hate it. They just used to cut the pig's throat. Then they would lay the pig on a big stone slab and shave all its hairs off.

Edna Vaughan was born at 8 Church Street.

85

My friend Edith was a Brotherton; we did everything together. I used to go in their house in the morning and the pig would be hung up with a bowl underneath to catch the blood. I can see him now, the man who killed the pigs; I used to hate him. He had a patch over one eye and his mouth went up at one corner. He used to give the bladder to the lads to play football.

Edna Vaughan

Rat-bags in charge

We used to go to the pictures at the Regal on the top of Rawmarsh Hill. We would walk up the back by Westfield Road to get there. On Saturday afternoon you could go to the matinee and that showed films just for kids. If you paid 7*d* you could sit at the front and if you were right rich you could pay 9*d* and sit at the back. Sometimes we would pay 7*d* and then try to crawl under the seats to the back, but there were really tough old women in charge – I am afraid to say we called them 'rat-bags' – who were really fierce and could remember who had bought 7*d* seats and who had bought 9*d* seats. They would drag you out and send you back down to the front. Occasionally someone would have broken the toilet window and then you might get in through that. A lot of the films we watched were ancient even then, ones with Flash Gordon and Hopalong Cassidy in.

Ray Hearne

Tom Jones in town

We used to play hopscotch, skipping, kick-can and snobs. I used to swim a lot at Rawmarsh Baths, often before and after school. There were three levels of diving boards there and I did dive then. I was good at swimming and swam for Yorkshire. I mainly swam with Ron Woodhouse and we are still friends. In the winter time the baths became a dance hall and planks were placed over the emptied pool to dance on. The floor did use to bounce when there were a lot of people dancing and we were only able to drink something like orange. The music was very varied; I saw Tom Jones there, as well as the Hollies, Dave Berry and Freddie and the Dreamers. I think it was someone called Les Slater who got all these groups. You didn't buy tickets in advance; you just got them on the door. We also went to the youth club at the Miners' Institute on Broad Street. There was a little tuck shop there where you could buy your sweets and drinks. It used to be really busy.

Yvonne Harrison

four

THE SECOND WORLD WAR

Joining up

About this time the Government were calling up lads at twenty for six months' training in case of war, so four of us decided to have a holiday. We went to the Cutler's Hall in Sheffield and we were given a choice of services. I decided on the Royal Navy, not being a great walker; I'd heard enough from my elder brother Ernest (Cufftee) Evans who was in the

Jim Evans on his wedding day during the Second World War.

army in the First World War. There were some right cases went for medicals. Herbert Riley chose the Royal Navy, but finished up in the Black Watch and was later taken prisoner at Hong Kong for the rest of the war. One came out of the medical room with a face as long as a fiddle. He wore a truss for a bad rupture and was medically exempt. One of the lads who didn't want to go asked if he could borrow the truss for his own examination. The doctor took one look at him and said 'M.E.'

'Medically exempt?' asked the chap,

'No,' said the doctor 'Middle East. If you can wear a truss upside down you can ride a camel!'

I was sent calling up papers to report to HMS *Royal Arthur* Training Depot at Skegness but I was a fortnight late going. When I did get there I looked like being shot having been absent without leave during war time and I wasn't even in the Royal Navy yet.

Jim Evans

Recalled from Ireland

I was in Ireland on holiday just before war was declared. I was out in the fields helping with the harvest when my aunt called me in because a telegram had arrived from my family. It said they had received a telegram from the West Riding telling all teachers to report into school the following Monday. The schools were to be opened to take the children, although not to teach as it was still the holidays. These were measures taken in preparation for war. I got a lift into Belfast and then I had to get a bus into the docks. Even then all the windows of the bus had been covered in tar and paint. The docks had been surrounded with barricades and security was really tight. I had to get on a boat carrying over a hundred eggs in two big tins. I always brought eggs back from my relatives in Ireland. I couldn't get a berth because I hadn't booked so I had to travel in the hold. Lots of soldiers were travelling back from Ireland so they were in the hold too. They put a tarpaulin over us and then started to sing so we had a concert all night.

When we landed, I got a train into Leeds and then one to Rotherham. It was early Sunday morning when I arrived. It was too early for a trackless so I walked from Masbrough into Rotherham. I was just walking past one of the houses in Masbrough when a chap rushed out and said war had just been declared. He had heard it on the radio. The barrage balloons were already up in Rotherham. I waited in All Saints' Square for the twelve o'clock bus to take me to Rawmarsh.

Evelyn Longden

Evelyn Longden was a local badminton and tennis champion as well as a primary school teacher.

3 September 1939

One Sunday morning we were in Sunday school at Rawmarsh, 3 September 1939, when the Sunday school superintendent, Mr Fenton, came into the school, went up onto the stage – which was a big one for concerts etc – and said that it had just been announced on the radio that war has been declared, and that we, Britain, are now at war with Germany. He offered a prayer and told us to go straight home. Brenda Brasher (later Senior) and I ran all the way home. We had no idea what to expect and I think we thought Hitler and

Joan Gillions was at Sunday school at the High Street Methodist Church when war was declared. Pictured here is the initial stone laying for the church in 1908.

his army were about to descend on us and shoot us. Anyway he didn't come. We carried on as normal at school, we practised ready for air raids and shelters were put up in our school fields for us all to go in when the air-raid sirens went off. It was a very eerie sound was the air-raid siren. We were all issued with a gas mask and we had to take it with us wherever we went. We were also issued with identity cards and ration books for food. Everyone was offered an air-raid shelter; back yards were full of them. This made it very difficult to dry the washing because the air-raid shelters took such a lot of space. We only went in our shelter twice, when it was the Sheffield Blitz.

Joan Gillions

Roll up and see a Messerschmitt

We were collecting money for planes and ships all through the war. We had Battle of Britain Days and plenty of others, with planes like Spitfires flying low over the trees.

No health and safety rules then! My dad took me up to Sheffield to Barker's Pool to see a Messerschmitt that had been shot down. They used to make a little charge to look at it and that's how they raised some money.

Albert Evans

After Dunkirk

After Dunkirk, all the houses round about where we lived in Green Lane were visited by officers with a view to billeting soldiers, two to a house if possible. Everybody pulled together on this. No. 199, Mrs Thorpe, had two sergeants; 203, Mrs Fowler, had two soldiers; mum and dad, 205, had two soldiers. There were six in the yard. Mrs Maye at 201 didn't have any soldiers, but she slept my brother Raymond. The soldiers had to be up early to parade at six or seven o'clock every morning on the grass across the road for drill and roll call etc. Then they were allowed free time to rest and gather their strength for a few weeks. They were all worn out and just had their uniforms and nothing else. The officers were billeted together across the road in a bungalow.

The top of Green Lane, close to where Joan Gillions has almost always lived.

The soldiers had ration books and extra food rations were available to people like my mum because we fed the troops. The strange thing about food during the war: plain food, not a lot of it, but I don't remember ever going hungry. Some children who were five or six years old at the end of the war had never seen a banana or a chocolate bar!

All the iron railings and gates were collected from the fronts of the houses, as well as pans, kettles; anything that could be melted down were collected up to be used for munitions. Remember, we in the UK were not prepared for war at all; Hitler was.

The blackout was something else. If there was no moon you couldn't see a thing outside. We used to count our footsteps off one pavement to the other side of the road. I once bumped my forehead on a lamp post and I had quite a lump for a few days. But when we had a moon it was marvellous.

Joan Gillions

Cooking in the WAFs

I joined up in Sheffield when I was eighteen – I joined the WAFs. I came home and told my dad that I had joined up as a cook and he burst out laughing. He said, 'you couldn't boil water without burning it!' But I learned and I ended up cooking for big numbers;

I've still got my book for cooking for a hundred men. I did my training in Bridgnorth, then Melsham and finally St Athens, before I was posted to Leconfield. It was a butchery course at St Athens; we were meant to be doing chops, but it ended up looking more like mincemeat! When I was at Leconfield we used to go to the Salvation Army, they were very good to us. We used to get a cup of tea and a bun if we joined in the singing.

Betty Watts

Betty Watts in her WAF uniform.

A group of WAFs on a cookery course and including Betty Watts.

A pennyworth of ABC sweets

During the war we had two soldiers billeted with us after Dunkirk. They were both from Kent I think. They used to send me and my friend Margaret Cooper to the shop to buy a pennyworth each of ABC sweets. This was before sweets were rationed. We had to make words up with them before we could eat them! They used to annoy me [the soldiers]; when the sirens went we always had to get up, but not them two. They stopped with us for most of one summer.

I can remember being in Mrs Reeve's class one afternoon and all of a sudden there was a terrible noise and it was the guns firing on Greasbrough Tops, so we had to go into the shelters; that would have been in 1940. There was a big gun at Thrybergh that was called Big Bertha. It was behind where the post office was. The man in charge there was Captain Pears and he was related to the soap people. He lodged with some of my relatives in a farmhouse in Hooton Roberts.

Freda Stacey

Pie first

My dad grew all his own vegetables. He had a big allotment at the back of the houses on Wheatcroft Road. It had been a field before the war. Our neighbours didn't want their

Joyce Bray (*née* Cooper) with her brother Geoffrey during the war.

allotment, so my dad took over that as well. I can remember picking vegetables at quarter to ten and dad was eating them by quarter past ten. We had plenty of veg but we were short of everything else. They put a big water tank on the waste ground across the road during the war to be used for fires if any bombs were dropped. We shared our Anderson shelter with the Read family so it was used for four adults and four children. The shelter was always damp and it had water in it, but we didn't go in very often. I can remember one night being in the shelter with planes going over and we kept shouting to mum, but she had to finish making a meat-and-potato pie before she'd come in. We were really worried. Dad organised the fire-watching rotas for our area and we had a board outside the house with the rotas for the street. He used to take a copy down to the council offices.

Joyce Bray

Working at Oxley's steelworks

I first started working at Oxley's in 1938; there were 120 people working there then. It was mainly forgings, foundry work and files. I started in the warehouse and then on to the foundry where I did the fettling. Our family originally came from Staffordshire. In the Second World War we made woodworking machinery for White's. Two of the directors then were Favell Oxley, who mainly worked on the financial side, and Mr South who lived in Swinton. Mr Oxley left after the war. We worked at least twelve hours a day then and there was fire-watching as well at Oxley's at night. I lived at the bottom of Willowgarth then and I was in the Home Guard at Brinsworth too. On the first day of the Sheffield Blitz I was called at 4 p.m. and the alert was still on at 6 the next morning. They reckon the blue language used by the Sergeant-Major, the Gunnery Officer, on Greasbrough Tops was so loud it could be heard on Rawmarsh Hill! All the pubs locally left their cellar doors open so they could be used as bomb shelters if needed.

George Hallam

George Hallam working with the Shell Moulding Machine at Oxley's.

Deaf to the Blitz

In the war I can remember going to the bomb site on Wentworth Road and collecting shrapnel. I went right down into the bomb crater. My grandfather, William Riley, who lived with us, had taken me there to see it. During the second night of the Sheffield Blitz some of the family were in Ryecroft Chapel when the raid started and my grandfather was worried when they failed to return. You could hear the shrapnel falling on the roof. He went to the chapel and found the preacher still preaching as he was deaf and hadn't heard the sound of the guns. He suggested everyone went to the shelters and a number came across to our cellar. We had an air-raid shelter dug in the garden, but we didn't use it because it used to fill up with water.

Our next-door neighbour was Mr Tingle and he worked in the woodworking part of the Chemical Works. He was able to get pieces of railway wagons to shore up both our cellars and knocked a hole through so we could talk to each other during a raid!

My grandfather refused to use either the shelter or the cellar, saying that they couldn't get him in the Boer War and they couldn't get him in the Great War, so they weren't likely to get him now. He just stayed in bed. He had served with the South Staffs in the Boer War and had come from Longton in Staffordshire to work at Roundwood Colliery.

Frank Horner

William Riley, Frank Horner's grandfather, who refused to go into an air-raid shelter.

Ready for giving the last rites

I'd been listening to Lord Haw-Haw on the radio during the week and he said that they were going to bomb Sheffield at the weekend. When I told other people this they told me not to be so silly. Being young, I thought it was exciting listening to him on the radio. I went to a dance in St Mary's Church Hall and it started while I was there. The siren went and of course it was all blacked out. Then the guns started firing on Greasbrough Tops. The dancing stopped and we stood around in the dimmed lights wondering what to do. The rector, Canon Scovell, came in, dressed in his white alb and carrying the communion things on a silver tray, ready for giving the last rites. He told us what it was for and frightened us all to death. I was in the Red Cross so I had to report at Rosehill School. I never had to treat anyone when I was in the Red Cross, but you had to be prepared.

Evelyn Longden

Grandpa's failing faith

We had an Anderson Shelter outside the back door of Sunnyside Cottage on a piece of grass. It was quite deep, with steps down to it. My grandpa lived across the road near the Council Yard. He didn't have a shelter, so we said he could use ours. One day when the sirens went he came across, but refused to go in the shelter; he said he would sit in the house and the Lord would protect him. We were in the shelter a long time and after the all-clear we went into the house looking for grandpa. Eventually we found him sitting on the cellar steps with his gas mask on. So much for trusting the Lord to protect him!

Mary Ferns

Working at Parkgate steelworks

During the war, production at the steelworks continued as before, but with air-raid shelters to go to if the sirens went off. It was during the war they started to serve meals in the works. Women were brought in to work in the mills, mainly as crane drivers. Most of them were local and they didn't seem to have to advertise much for them. Parkgate then seemed very family-orientated and most of the women workers were probably related to steelworkers there in some way or other. There was no bad feeling about the women working there; most of the men seemed to welcome the fact that they were working with women! There were all sorts of stories about the night shift but we won't go into that!

Henry Lowry

A woman driving one of the small locomotives in Parkgate steelworks during the war.

Supporting the war effort

When war was declared in 1939, young and old who were not eligible for active service were requested to support the war effort in a number of different ways as befitted their ability. I was asked to collect pennies for the Red Cross 'Penny a Week Fund' and my mother sold National Savings Stamps on Albert Road where we lived. Each Saturday morning I set out with my collecting tin and walked the length of the street, knocking on doors, chatting with the elderly, avoiding barking dogs and talking to the children who were invariably on the look-out for me, pennies in hand. Two such I remember were Nina Underwood and her sister Pat (now Bennett). When hostilities ended, I finally said farewell to my tin for the last time. I eventually received a signed photograph of the Duke of Gloucester (the queen's uncle and patron of the Red Cross) and a letter of appreciation stating that I and the people of Albert Road had contributed, with thousands of others, in raising £50 million for the war effort.

Marian Overland

Albert Road, where Marian Overland went collecting pennies for the Red Cross.

Wartime wedding

I worked as a shorthand typist at Steel, Peech and Tozer's not long after I left school. I was there eleven years in all and eventually, as it was wartime, I had to get permission to leave to look after my parents. All the family, including me, were in reserved occupations during the war. I got married at the old chapel in Ryecroft. The first night of my marriage we spent in the cellar because that was the night they bombed Sheffield. We had the reception in a hotel on Moorgate and we had just finished our meal when the management came and said there was an air raid coming. They offered us the use of their cellar, but we decided to go home to Rawmarsh instead.

Nellie Schofield

Clegg's Cottage bombed

Clegg's Cottage stood at the junction of Wentworth Road and Blackamoor Road. It was eventually demolished about 1948. It used to be called the 'Salthouse'. It was a whitewashed cottage and was called the 'Salthouse' because when the carriers and their

A painting of Clegg's Cottage by Freda Stacey's father. The only German bombs to land in Rawmarsh in the Second World War fell close to this cottage where the Badgers lived.

packhorses came from Cheshire with the salt they used to leave some there for the local farmers. The farmers needed some blocks for their animals to lick.

My grandfather and grandmother used to live in Clegg's Cottage and they were living there during the Second World War. One night in the war, in the early hours of the morning, the watchers up at the post just behind the Woodman Inn saw a single plane fly over and drop two bombs near Wentworth Road. Mr Malpass was on duty and he said, 'Bill Badger will have had it,' as the bombs landed close to Clegg's Cottage. They all made their way down Blackamoor and they could see the house was still standing, but there was no sign of anyone. The door of the cottage was unlocked as usual so they went in. They found my Grandfather Bill and Grandmother Clara inside, sitting by the fire, and everything, including them, was totally covered in soot. They must have been suffering from shock. Mr Malpass said, 'All right, Bill?' and he replied 'I've been trying to sweep that bloody chimney for thirty odd years and that b★★★★r from Berlin had to come over and do it for me.' I went down the following day with the family and we were running round the bomb crater looking for shrapnel. One bomb had dropped right next to the road and the other about 20 yards into the field. Grandfather went up to Warren House Farm and told the farmer to cover over the two big piles of lime he had in his field with muck as he reckoned they would have looked like two big bell tents from the air. He really played the devil with that farmer. He also got the family to cover his whitewashed walls with tar to hide it better.

Harold Badger

Pub with no beer

Opposite Dale Road School there was a little sweet shop owned by Pharaoh Bostock. During the war he used to allocate his sweets carefully, even down to the last three humbugs. He got a fridge and started making his own ice pops and selling them, until the health people got to hear of it. He'd run out of sticks so he started to make his own like the sort we sold for people's fires! He used to live with his mum and he never got married.

Pub opening then was twelve till two and seven till ten. There was generally not enough money nor time for many people to get really drunk, even if there was plenty of singing. Four Lane Ends did have a bit of a reputation for being a place where drunks did end up scrapping. In the war pubs did run out of beer and signs were put up reading 'Sorry No Beer Tonight'. At times they sold 'red biddy' at the Station Hotel at Aldwarke.

John Turner

No memories of bananas

During the Second World War we had a register of customers to cope with the rationing. Onions, oranges and dried peas were all rationed and I've no memories of bananas at all. We used to collect rhubarb from Wakefield way, but we shouldn't have really because it was too far to travel. We were in a pig club run by the Brothertons, who lived down Church Street. They used to collect swill in a bins fixed to a trailer behind a car. The pigs were fattened up and killed at Christmas. They used to put grease and saltpetre on the cuts of pork hung up, to preserve them I think. We kept eggs in 'glass water' and they kept well. We also kept tomatoes in bottles.

Bryan Ward

Bryan and Helena Ward on honeymoon in London. The Ward's greengrocery business was very well known in Rawmarsh and Parkgate.

A cosy billet

When Philip, my future husband, joined up he went to Sheffield at first to work with the barrage balloons and then they were posted to Parkgate and he was asked to pick the best site. There was one at Newbiggin, a few others and then one at Mangham. He decided on Mangham because he knew someone in the Chemical Works nearby who could get them coke for their fire, he knew he could also get someone who worked on the railway from Stubbin pit that ran nearby to throw out some bits of coal on to the bank near the balloons and he knew he could get himself billeted at his home on Broad Street where his parents ran a fish and chip shop. Philip used to go home to get some potatoes and some fat and then they used to fry some chips on their fire. They were there until the WAFs took over the balloons. When they first brought the big guns to put on Greasbrough Tops they had to move them because they started sinking into some coal working below. They even lost some horses there I think. They put up some huts there for the people on the guns to live. After the war the huts got squatters in them; people who had nowhere else to live.

I came home from the forces on 4 September 1945. We had got married in June before the war was over. Philip's family, the Watts, got fish for the chip shop all the way through the war and the fish cost 16s a stone. The problem was the fat was rationed. They used to get their fat, called Snowdrift, from Bailey's before the war. Mr Bailey said to Philip's dad

The barrage balloon station on Mangham Lane where Philip Watts initially served in the war.

before the war 'Mr Watts there's going to be a war so get some extra fat now because it's bound to be rationed and it will be allocated on what you buy now'. That way they had enough in the war.

Betty Watts

Joining the Land Army

I used to like to go to the Baths for the Saturday Night Hop. No ruffians like nowadays! Towards the end of the war I met Thelma Waldron there and she was in the Land Army. I said I wouldn't mind going in the Land Army and she said she would ask Mrs Watson, who she worked for, if I could join them. Mrs Watson agreed to me starting there and I began as a civilian. Then I applied for the Land Army and I went to see Mrs Langdon, that's Colonel Langdon's wife, who was in charge of Wentworth Woodhouse at that time. She agreed to me signing up and to continue working at the Watson's Farm.

The farm was at Droppingwell and was run by Mr and Mrs Watson, although Mr Watson seemed more involved with a red shale quarry down at Bradgate. There were six of us girls working at the farm and we were all local. We all got on like a house on fire. There was me, Thelma Waldron and her sister from Blythe Avenue, Evelyn Havenhand from Canklow, Doreen Cook from Bradgate and Dora Noble from Middle Lane. We all lived at home and I used to go by bus every day. We took sandwiches and a flask for lunch every day and we ate it in a garden shed with no heating of any description. We wore donkey-brown coats and hats. We had a lot of jobs on the farm, but the most important one was milking the Friesian cows. We milked them at about 7.30 a.m. and 5 p.m. every day.

Edna Pease in her Land Army uniform.

We also had to feed hay to the cows, but mucking out was the worst. It was really bad if the cows had eaten some potatoes! I used to be embarrassed getting on the bus at night sometimes because of the muck on my clothes.

We had a weekend off once a fortnight. When we did work the weekend we had to go Sunday morning and put three churns of milk into the back of Mr Watson's car and it was brought into Rotherham. We also made hay stoups, fed the bull and looked after the two big cart horses (one was called Paul). Thelma used to drive the tractor. Threshing was one of the worst jobs; you had to put something round your face because the dust was so bad. One day, we had to take the cows up to the main road and across to another field. As we got to the road there were three big lorries full of American troops coming down Wortley Road. They were all whistling at us, but we had to stop them to get the cows across.

I got paid £2 10s a week in the Land Army. I carried on working there for two and a half years, but then I had to leave to look after my mother. Dr O'Connell at Parkgate helped to get me out of the Land Army. He was my mother's doctor.

My husband, Fred Pease, worked at Kilnhurst pit, but he was called up and served in the Royal Ordnance Corps. He served down at the Sunderland flying boats base at Pembroke Dock. He told me once about a 'Gerry' plane coming over and attacking the base and machine-gunning and killing some of the soldiers who were on the parade ground. He 'dove' under a wash-basin in the latrines and survived. He was called back to the pit soon after because he was needed there, even though he wanted to stop in the army.

Edna Pease

Training in the USA

I was sent to London to start off with, to train for the RAF. I was in a block of flats and there were seven others in my room and all the rest were Londoners and were quite posh. There was me with my broad Yorkshire accent – it amused them no end. One said to me, 'Now then Yorkie, what are you going to do now we've got the weekend off? ' I had no plans as there was nowhere to go. So he rang his mother and arranged for me to go home with him. They lived in a lovely flat and they made me very welcome. She said she had prepared a special dish for me and brought out a Yorkshire pudding. The only trouble was it was covered with sugar and currants!

I got sent abroad for some of my training. We got on board a ship named *The Andes* and I thought we were going to South Africa. We went at twenty-seven knots and ended up in Halifax in Canada. We couldn't believe the amount of food in the canteen and there were barrels of tea, coffee and milk to serve yourself. Then they allocated us to flying schools. I thought I had chosen to go to Miami, but it was actually Miama in Oklahoma. We trained in small aeroplanes at first and then we went on to Harvards. All the pilots training us were Americans. They were all ever so friendly and didn't bother much with saluting. The local people were very good to us too; we never had to buy ourselves any meals all the time we were there. In all I was there nine months. I came back to England then and was allocated to flying Lancaster bombers, an airman's delight. By this time it was quite close to the end of the war. We did raids over Germany, but we were surrounded by loads of American Mustang planes so we were never attacked.

Ted Frost

Ted Frost being presented with his RAF wings after training in the USA.

I did fire twice

I joined the Home Guard when I was sixteen and the church in Hollybush was our headquarters. I played football for them and if you played they used to feed you. Usually we just pretended to use a gun or throw a grenade, but I did fire six rounds twice; once at a firing range in the church and once up at a big house at Ravenfield.

Cliff Hawley

Planes over Rawmarsh

One thing I will never forget, during the light nights when the 1,000 bomber raids took place over Germany, is the planes going over looked like swarms of flies in the sky. They were very, very high. The sky was full of them, the constant drone, drone, drone. My Grandma Uttley would stand on the step and cry and say 'Somebody's lads will not come home again', and of course she was right. We feared for the pilots and we also feared for the people in Germany who would soon be killed.

Then on 8 May 1945 peace was declared. What a wonderful, wonderful day – singing, street parties; everyone gave everything they could muster. No more blackout, but it was a very long time before everything got back to normal. Gradually the soldiers and all the men in the forces were demobbed; some had been six years away, like Eddie, my cousin, and Jack, my other cousin. They were both twenty-two when they joined up and twenty-eight when they were demobbed. Food filtered back very slowly. Also very slowly rations were increased. It was a few years before food rationing finished.

Joan Gillions

Putting my life on the line

I got demobbed in London having taken early release and I had to come home and return to the same job I had before I signed up. I went along to Stubbin pit and got a job as a cutter with my brother-in-law Chris Ward. I went down the pit and Chris was in charge of the cutter and I was behind it. The seam we were in was only about 3ft high and I got all the dust at the back of the cutter. I didn't last long.

I can remember going into the Travellers pub in Parkgate one night not long after I got home and there were all these POWs there from the camp up on Greasbrough Tops. They had to wear a special sort of uniform with an orange patch on the back. I couldn't believe it and there were the local people buying them drinks! I thought this was very strange –

there had I been fighting these b★★★★rs and here were people buying them drinks. This was happening even though money was scarce then. Later I also saw loads of local young girls hanging around the wire fence of the POW camp on Greasbrough Tops chatting up the prisoners. I had put my life on the line to beat them and here they were being chatted up and getting free drinks.

Ted Frost

POWs and St Joseph's, Rawmarsh

Father O'Donoghue was parish priest at St Joseph's, Green Lane, during and after the war. I suppose he went up to the POW camp on Greasbrough Tops as a priest. His nephew, Sean Martin, helped out in the parish as well. After the war, in 1946, the prisoners were allowed out of the camp and some came to Mass with a guard. They had a lovely choir and Miss Adiss played the organ. At Christmas, Father O'Donoghue asked the parishioners if anyone could invite any of the POWs for Christmas dinner. My mum and dad ended up

Children at St Joseph's involved in the May Queen parade.

inviting four or five of them and they carried on calling on us afterwards. They generally spoke quite good English and the ones who visited us had been in the German army. One, I remember, had been an architect in Berlin before the war. At least one of them married a local girl when he was released. Another of the prisoners worked on a farm in Thrybergh and became so friendly with the family that he got invited to the wedding of the farmer's daughter. He had to borrow some clothes from my brother as he had nothing to wear.

The low category prisoners were kept at Rawmarsh and the high category ones were at Lodge Moor in Sheffield. I don't think they went back till 1948 because I can remember them digging out the roads and pavements after all the snow in the winter of 1947. Before they left, the prisoners made everyone in our family a pair of dyed hessian slippers as a farewell present.

Helena Ward

Black Market in a time of rationing

One day, when rationing was still on after the war, I went in my brother Donald's van to Palfreyman's farm at Bolton-upon-Dearne. I saw him take two milk churns into the farm and he came out a bit later with two churns and loaded them back in the van. We were on

A view of High Street showing the side of Downs' butchers shop. The churns filled with illicit pork were brought to some outbuildings here by the Turner brothers.

Coley Lane when he became suspicious that we were being followed. He told me to get into the back of the van and if the car behind pulled up in front of us I was to open the doors at the back from inside and push the churns out so that hopefully they would roll into the ditch. Luckily it was a false alarm and we got back to the dairy safely. [Donald was a cowman at Ronnie Shaw's farm at Haugh and he had a little dairy in the outbuildings of Downs' butchers shop, close to the Regal Cinema. He bought a milk round off Ronnie Shaw and ran it as a separate business.] When we got the churns out of the van I found out they were full of joints of pork! That's what it was like then with rationing after the war. There was one local butcher or slaughterhouse worker called Bell who used to walk around in his overcoat with all the tools of his trade inside his coat! If a pig had been 'knocked down' he would come and butcher it.

John Turner

Dining out in Green Lane

We had two street parties at the end of the war and then there were tables down the middle of the street. We had games for the children later in the evening. Mr Staves's father lived in Wheatcroft Road and gave prizes for different things. I won half a crown for singing. Even then he took his fruit and veg round on a lorry. In the war we used to go to Schonhut's in Parkgate and get some roast pork in gravy. You had to take a basin to put it in. For lunch on a Saturday we used to go to the National Restaurant – that was in Green Lane straight opposite Barber's Avenue. The actual restaurant building is still used but it is now in Rockcliffe Road. The menu was meat and veg at the restaurant followed by a pudding. You did not have to use coupons for them and they were cheap. They were always very busy.

There was a barrage balloon at the end of New Street coming down to the avenues. Everybody used to help each other during the war. No one was really on their own.

While I was at Haugh School in the war I went to Bewley Park Camp for a month, that's at Pateley Bridge. We went there to a school so we had lessons during the morning, but then in the afternoons we were round and about doing nature studies. I'd never been away from home before. It was only children from our school that were at the camp at that time. They organised games and things for the evening. After two weeks our mothers had a trip out to meet us. We went to the pictures in Pateley Bridge; it only cost us about 2*d* or 3*d*. For holidays at home we mainly went to Rosehill Park, although we did go to Clifton Park occasionally. There were lots of fund raising events during the war collecting money for the Red Cross, the air force etc. Everybody was knitting. There were special Savings Weeks at school as well.

Joyce Bray

five

WORK

Until the street was clear

My aunty, Betty Daffin, worked for Atkinson's the drapers at the beginning of the twentieth century. Atkinson's shop was at the bottom end of Parkgate on Broad Street. She told me on Saturdays they had to work until midnight and before they were allowed to go home Mr Atkinson would go outside and look up and down Broad Street and if he could see anyone there, they weren't allowed home until the street was clear and he was sure he hadn't got another customer! I think they finished at ten o'clock during the week.

Margaret Chambers

Pony driver at Aldwarke

At the age of thirteen I got a job at a local colliery; to get the job I had to tell them I was fourteen. My first weekly wage for a six-day week, eight hours a day, was 7*s* 6*d*. I started as a lamp carrier, which were oil lamps in those days. A lamp carrier had to carry six spare lamps to a manhole not far from the coal face and wait for someone to call for another. The next job I had was a door trapper. This was done on a roadway where tubs were drawn to the pit bottom by ropes and there were doors for ventilation purposes. Later I became a pony driver at Aldwarke Main Colliery.

The seam of coal was the Swallow Wood seam, about 4ft thick, a very good quality and hard steam coal, which was got out by hand. The length of the face was about 20 yards, enough for two colliers and a trammer. At that time it was very hard to work in the pits; the coal was so hard it had to be split into lumps with wedges and hammers. It took two miners as long as eight hours to fill two ten-hundredweight tubs and over two weeks to get the whole 20 yards of coal ready for dropping. My pony had to either pull a tub of coal or hold back a tub on an incline. The tubs were wooden with iron strips to hold them together. I worked in the district called the Old Dips and there were five other districts, all very steep inclines.

In 1912 I got my first introduction to a strike; it was called the 'Pony Drivers' Strike'. Six local pits came out on strike for about 6*d* a week more. The pits involved were two at Aldwarke, Roundwood, Silverwood and two in Rotherham. 1913 arrived with a rise in my wage at the pit, I received my first gold half sovereign and a three pence 'joey', that was a silver threepenny piece. The odd threepence paid my union. These were bad days and we did not know where the next meal would come from. We did not get our wages until we finished our Saturday shift at two o'clock. My father's job was in danger as the coal seams were getting worked out and there were no prospects for the future. We never had a holiday, although I did used to walk from Parkgate to Rotherham to see Rotherham County and Rotherham Town play football on alternate weeks. I watched Rotherham County when they won the Midland League four seasons in succession.

Leslie Evans

Les Evans is shown on the right of this photograph in his army uniform from the First World War. He posed for this picture with two of his brothers, Norman and Ossie.

Chemical Cottages

There were two cottages at Chemical Cottages, a lot of outbuildings and a greenhouse. Their addresses were 5 and 6 Wentworth Road. There were two houses about 300 yards away from the cottages further into Birchwood, down near the stream. There was a pond in front of the cottages where a stream had been dammed up. They needed a lot of water because there was a dye-works there owned by two brothers called White. They got the dyes from the trees nearby; they were called wood naphtha. My uncle lived there once and he said it used to be a thriving little industry employing several workers including draymen. The cottages had no tap water or gas, but they did have a well. The well water they only used for washing, and for drinking water they went up to Clegg's Cottage with their buckets to use the outside tap.

Harold Badger

These thatched cottages were originally known as Chemical Cottages. They were replaced later by a brick building. The dyeing business may have started in these older buildings.

Joseph Morris as sexton

There used to be a one-up one-down cottage at the old cemetery on the High Street and that was part of the original sexton's house. My grandfather, Joseph Morris, was sexton and eventually caretaker there. I grew up hearing stories of him walking in front of the coffin to a burial and wearing his frock coat. When his wife died, around 1933, my parents and I moved into Cemetery House to look after grandad. He was obviously a well-known and much respected person.

Mary Hutchinson

The General Strike

In 1926, during the strike, my old man used to take me coal picking on Stubbin tip; I was only eight at the time. We used to go up Haugh Lane and down a track to Bank Cottages, which was pretty steep, and pulling a barrow of coal up was no joke. He used to tie me to the barrow for two reasons: one to help him pull and two so that I couldn't run off! This barrow was a home-made effort, about 6ft long and 3ft wide with wheels off old wringing machines or mangles as they were called. The axle was made by 'Old Footit', the blacksmith at the top of Pottery Street.

Jim Evans

Shallow pits

During the General Strike my grandma told me that coal was short and my uncle dug a small pit near my grandma's house in Victoria Road to get some coal. There were some steps down from a yard to get into the pit. Everyone had to keep quiet when the police came round so they didn't hear any digging. They often did the mining at night to avoid the police catching them and the pits were that shallow you could hear the men working from inside the houses. Cliff's mum and dad actually sold coal from their pit, which was nearby. Lorries used to come to collect the coal they got so much. Cliff's mum said she never had so much money as when she was selling the coal then. Victoria Road must have been like a rabbit warren underground.

When I left school at fourteen my first job was at Woolworth's in Rotherham and then later I worked as a receptionist at a dentist's in Corporation Street in Rotherham. After two years I was bored because I didn't have enough work to do, so I went in the Land Army. Marrion, my sister, was already in. I was a tractor driver at a farm in Skipton. I stopped there for two years. I came home every weekend because we had started courting by then and we used to go to the pictures or to a dance. I left the Land Army after two years.

Joyce Hawley

Climbing the job ladder

I started work in 1927 at Parkgate steelworks when I was fifteen. I stayed on at school for a time because of the coal strike linked to the General Strike and there wasn't much work around. I worked a bit like a secretary at the school for that time, this was at Netherfield Lane. Clem White was the headmaster there. At the steelworks I started as an errand boy in Number 2 mill, that was a plate mill, and I got 8*s* 9*d* a week at first. I also got 2*d* an hour extra on a Saturday if I worked between twelve and one. I gave my two younger sisters a penny each from that.

There were four plate mills then and Number 2 mill was the modern one. Sometimes they would roll Staybrite in Number 2 mill, which was a special steel. The plates were

sent off, mainly by rail, to aeroplane companies and a few still to shipyards. They were loaded on at Parkgate or Aldwarke stations. The sidings for the steelworks came later. Some of the production was exported then. They were making armour plating in Number 2 mill before the war started in 1939. The shears were used to cut the plates exactly to the right size for the orders. There would be about thirty men working on each shift in Number 2 mill at that time. My job changed to a weigh-boy after a bit. Then I moved to the 10in and later the 18in mill. In both of these the steel was fed in by men with tongs and caught at the other end and sent back. Workers had to move the molten bars across the mill floor by rolling it with their feet. They wore clogs with a metal strip on the bottom and used these to move the bars that

Henry Lowry as a young man.

A scene from inside the Parkgate steelworks where Henry Lowry spent much of his working life.

Thousands of men were employed at Parkgate steelworks, including these photographed in the 1920s.

were 70–80ft long. Later I was a shift foreman at the 24in mill. In that mill we made a lot of joists, props and arches for collieries. In the smaller mills they made fish plates for joining the props and arches together. We used to roll rails in the 24in mill as well.

Henry Lowry

Walked from Jarrow

We knew a man called Jim Kirk who had walked down to Parkgate all the way from Jarrow to get a job. This must have been in the 1920s. He got a job as the head roller at Parkgate forge. His daughter Dorothy was a teacher and Guide captain at the parish church. She used to arrange trips for us from the church all over, to places like London and the Isle of Wight, and we used to stop in youth hostels. This would have been in the years after the war.

A visit to London by a group from the parish church and led by Miss Kirk. Included in this image are; Sheila Skeldon, Betty Turner, Betty Gostling, Mary Garbutt and Marian Davis.

John Skeldon, who was a local teacher, was my cousin, although he was quite a bit older than me. His father, Jim, started working for Pugh's, the builders. John's sister, Alice, was also a teacher and she married Harry Grundy. Harry's mother came from Germany, apparently moving with the Schonhuts as a maid when they came across. Harry had a beautiful voice and sang locally, but he was probably good enough to have been a professional.

Sheila Skeldon

Working at the Kilnhurst Co-op

I started work when I was fourteen at the Kilnhurst Co-op; it was my first job. I worked from half-past eight in the morning till six in the evening with an hour for lunch. Lunchtime was between one and two, but any customers in the shop you had to serve before you started your dinner. I lived in Ryecroft then and walked to work because there were no buses. I left the house at eight o'clock. I worked upstairs with one other person, then there were two on the hosiery counter, two on the drapery counter and two in the shoe shop. Then they extended it and we had two in the basement where we sold lino, there were two in the furniture shop, two in confectionery and two in the chemist's. The groceries were delivered by horse and cart and we had three lorries as well. Jack

Kilnhurst Co-op, where Muriel Sykes worked for many years.

Deardon, Mr Hawke and Sid Hargreaves were on deliveries. Drapery orders went out on different days to different places. We delivered to Dalton, to Sunnyside, all over. Two lads worked in the flour department weighing up and bagging up the flour for sale. Mr Frost worked on the bacon counter and Mr Charles went out for orders. He also worked in a little office on orders and pricing the groceries. There was also a Mr Woolfinden on the counter. Most of our supplies came by rail. Most of the customers came on the train as well as there were no buses to Kilnhurst when I first started working in the 1920s.

Muriel Sykes

My time in the Isolation Hospital

In August 1930, when I was four, I caught diphtheria. My brother had died from it not long before. They took me to the Isolation Hospital at Rosehill and Dr Menzies had to perform an emergency tracheotomy on me on the kitchen table to keep me alive. I was kept in a room by myself so I didn't infect anyone else and the nurses were always boiling kettles to keep the atmosphere moist. At that time Nurse Brooksbank and Nurse Oxley worked there and the matron was Elizabeth Ellis. When I was getting better I can remember jumping up and down on the bed and copying the nurses by shouting, 'On duty'. I think it was this experience that made me want to be a nurse when I left school. To be a nurse you had to have had all your vaccinations, but my dad never agreed with vaccination, he said that there was no need for all that filth in your body. I wanted to be a nurse so I had to be vaccinated secretly. One funny thing I can remember from being young in Rawmarsh was that the fever ambulance was black and if you saw it going past, you spat on your finger and put a cross on the sole of your shoe!

Joan Pearce

Saturday night till eleven

I left school before I was fourteen because my birthday is in August. I went straight into the family business in Ward's fruit shop. At that time there were very long hours. In the week we were open till eight or nine and Friday night would be later. Saturday night you were open till after the second house at the pictures, so till gone eleven. We had to polish up the brass weights with Brasso and black lead the scales. Then I saw a job advertised at the Co-op in Rotherham and I got it. The hours there were much better.

Marjorie Oxer

Ward's greengrocers shop on Stocks Lane, where Marjorie Oxer started work.

Accident pay

My grandad, Charlie Clarkson, worked in the colliery till he was seventy-five and was ninety-nine when he died. One Saturday he broke two ribs getting the coal in at home. My grandmother strapped him up and he managed to get through the Sunday and he took the strapping off and went to work on Monday morning. When he had been at work a couple of hours he pretended to have an accident so that then he could be paid his 1s 6d a week as he had been hurt at work, otherwise he would have got nothing.

The Clarksons were Rawmarsh people, but my grandmother was from Kingswinford. She came over here to look after her cousin Sarah Lancashire, who'd just had a baby. My grandma always kept a few lumps of coal near the back door so that if my mother cheeked her and ran away she had something to throw at her!

Noreen Brown

Making wreaths

My mother used to make wreaths and crosses, being so close to the churchyard and the cemetery. At that time about 5*s* was the price of a wreath. One day a woman came from Swinton and said she wanted a chaplet – that was a special wreath wired in the shape of a heart. She didn't come to collect it and as the time of the funeral approached she asked me and Roy Edwards, from Craven Yard across the road, to get on a trolley and take it to Swinton. She didn't want to miss out on being paid. We got off at the church just as the hearse arrived so we had to stop it and get the chaplet put on the coffin. Someone did come to pay for it afterwards.

There used to be a little yard next to the old Regal cinema called Moxon's Yard and Mrs Moxon and old Mr Moxon lived there. They used to make piccalilli in a big pot and I used to go and buy it from them. It was only a house shop and she sold it out of a little window. You used to get three-penn'orth or a pennyworth. Anyway old Mr Moxon died and the family came to buy some wreaths. I had to take them across. When I went, Mrs Moxon said did I want to look at him, so I said yes. She took me into the parlour and there on a sort of table he was laid in a coffin and I thought he looked a lot better than he had when he was alive. He looked so pink and white. I would have been about seven then.

Mary Ferns

Top secret

For years my father kept secret from my mother how much he earned every week. Eventually my mother found a pay packet in his coat pocket with his name and wage written on it. She couldn't believe how much it was. They didn't speak to each other for donkey's years after that.

Ted Frost

Family job

There were a lot of three-generation steelworkers. My dad and his dad had worked at the Parkgate works before me and I had several uncles working there as well. When you applied for a job they asked for a reference, but that was really only a formality; if your relatives were good workers you were in.

They always used to say that the way to get on at Parkgate was to either go to chapel or to play cricket for Aldwarke Park (they played close to the site of Aldwarke Hall).

Work in the steelworks in Gordon Read's early days was still arduous and potentially very dangerous.

This was when Sir Harry Williams was in charge. Discipline in the works then was good. My grandad told me that earlier people had been laid off in the 1930s when Freddy Woodifield used to walk round and if he caught anyone not working he would send them down to the office to collect their cards.

Gordon Read

Some of the workforce at Parkgate steelworks including Isaac Uttley. Note all the sweat towels and sweat caps.

Work a week, lake a week

When I was fourteen I started work at New Stubbin Colliery and the first few days were a bit rough. The older lads used to play all kinds of tricks on you, but after a while I was as bad as the rest. I stopped at Stubbin till about 1935 and times were bad; work a week, lake a week. We used to listen for the buzzer at half-past eleven; if it went there was no work for the afternoon shift, so I packed up and got a job at Sheffield Steel Products.

Jim Evans

Jack, Jim and Ernest Evans: three brothers enjoying a drink.

Working at Oxley's

There was still crucible steel melting when I started and that involved picking up 56lb crucibles with pincers. One of the workers called 'Pot Jack' made the crucibles with clay in a mould. They stopped using crucibles sometime between the end of the war and 1950. The file making was split between men and women with men making the files and women working as file cutters. I can always remember the smell of hot metal hitting the wet moulded sand. Later, we went on to carbon-dioxide moulding called 'blackwash'. Wooden patterns were made out of plywood and Jack Potts was the pattern maker. He was very particular about his tools; he used to lay them out really carefully. One day someone used one of his chisels to sharpen a pencil, he nearly walked out! Some of the patterns were 8 or 9ft long and they used to be sprayed with flour before sand was put round them to leave them clean. There were eight workers in the foundry and three or four in the melting team. George Snellson was one of the moulders and Raymond Sanderson was his 'boy'.

George Hallam

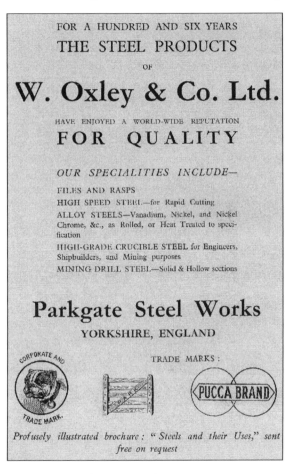

An advertisement for the products of Oxley's steelworks, which was already over a hundred years old when this was printed.

Miner not joiner

I always wanted to be a joiner and I had got a job lined up, but my dad put my name down for the pit at fourteen and that was that. This was because you got paid 2s more as a miner than a joiner and my dad wanted the extra money. We were really poor because of my dad and my mother knew we were often starving. We only had two chairs in our house

Cliff and Joyce Hawley on their wedding day in 1950.

so for meals all the children had to stand up. One day mother went up to my dad's pigeon loft and threw in a cat to kill all the birds. She told my dad that he was spending money on feeding them when his own children were starving. The Simpsons were the dominant family on the Island, as the area around Infirmary Road was called, and my mother was related to them. You only got a house on the Island if the Simpsons said so.

Cliff Hawley

Teaching in Low End, Parkgate

When I taught at Rotherham Road after the war I went to see a family in Stanley Street about one of their boys running off from school and crossing the railway lines to get to the canal. An older brother was on probation in Wakefield but he kept coming home and taking his brother out of school. They were a very poor family. When the older one came to school dinners at first he stood at the table to eat. I told him to sit down saying, 'Haven't you got any chairs in your house?' One of the other children piped up, 'No they haven't got any chairs, Miss'. When I went in the house they had no doors or door frames, they had all gone on the fire. The same had happened to the floorboards – there was just soil for the floors of the rooms downstairs. The boys had made a hole in the ceiling so they could slide down a rope from their bedroom to the kitchen. The baby slept in a bottom drawer. The mother was a fat and comfortable woman and said to me, 'Eh don't you worry about them, love. They went missing last week and I found them on top of that mountain off Rotherham Road [the tip heap near the old Recreation Ground]; they'd been camping there all night.'

Evelyn Longden

Scrapping on the coal belts

I left school at fourteen. My dad had a good job at Parkgate steelworks as a second hand. My dad wanted me to work at Parkgate forge but I didn't want to. I wanted to go to Stubbin pit because I had mates working on the pit top or in the pit. I knew I could get more money in the pit too. My dad argued, but I stuck it out.

I started working on the pit top as most young lads did. We stood on either side of a moving belt picking the dross out of the coal as it went towards the wagons. There was a lad opposite me and we never got on. We used to finish up scrapping on these belts. The boss on the top there said, 'If you b******s don't stop you're going down the bloody pit.' Next day we were at it again, so we had to go down the pit. There was a big, lean and muscular charge hand down there who didn't stand any messing about. If you did anything wrong he would come up behind and squeeze the back of your leg and it was really painful. I was working with my mate Jack Machin. We went into the Thorncliffe Seam eventually. There was a steep slope on the road down to it. Jack used to drive an air engine down there and later I did too.

When the war started they would limit the number of miners who went in the baths at any one time in case a bomb came down. I got fed up with this and decided to join the RAF. By this time I was sixteen and a half. My dad was dead against it and I was too young, but I volunteered when I was seventeen. I was accepted but my maths wasn't good enough so I had to go to evening classes at Ashwood Road and finally signed up at eighteen.

Ted Frost

Back to Civvy Street

Back to civilian life with an L96 and a new demob suit from Laws in Parkgate. We spent the L96 at Cantors on furniture because all we had was a bed at our old man's; we were lodgers. I went back to my old job at Mines Rescue where the manager was Mr Saul, or Major Saul; he won his rank in the Home Guard. The money at work wasn't much a week, in fact I don't think they'd had a raise all through the war.

Jim Evans

Frozen pipes

I can remember the winter of 1947. I seemed to be working twenty-five hours a day because I was a plumber so there was lots of work with frozen pipes. I think there was snow on the ground from February right up to early May. It was a terrible winter with all the ice on the road and all the frozen ruts.

Reg Ferns

Reg Ferns, who was worked off his feet in 1947 at the height of the Big Freeze.

I learned to swear

I started off at Parkgate steelworks as a trainee on the staff side. I got paid £2 12s 6d for my first week's wage. That was 2s 6d more than the office boys got. That was in 1951. As a trainee you spent so many weeks in each department and you had to write an essay on each placement. One of the places I had to go was in the 12in bar mill. I realised there that I could earn anything up to £6 a week working on the shop floor so I asked to come off the staff. After a struggle and an argument they allowed me to.

Initially I was drawing billets out of the furnace. The assistant furnace man had a large pair of tongs attached to a chain and I helped him by opening the furnace door. Then I had to bring a transfer table across for the billet to be loaded on it. I had to be careful or I would nip the fingers of the assistant furnace man (who was Verdi Coucom), but I did not

always get it right. That was where I learned to swear! The billet was then transferred onto the roller gear and went into the first set of rolls. When I went in the shift pattern started Sunday night and was continuous production through to Saturday afternoon, but as demand increased it went on to a full twenty-four-hour rota, seven days a week. The 12in mill opened in 1935 and closed in the mid-1970s.

I moved on to be a fourth helper before becoming an assistant charger. Promotion was quite rapid as people were leaving to do their National Service. I went into the forces at eighteen and came out two years later and of course my old job was waiting for me, but by then I had decided I wanted to get back on the staff; I didn't want to sweat any more. When I left school at sixteen I weighed 10st

Gordon Read as a 12-year-old in his uniform from Mexborough Grammar School.

6lbs and after two years' work I was 10st 4lbs. My first three months in the forces saw my weight rise to 12st. That was mainly the effect of sweating less. We used to drink lots of water and take salt tablets. I also drank beer. The 'slagger' would go out on the afternoon shift to collect beer. He was given a 'pass-out' to leave the works and took bottles to be filled and money, usually to the Rail Mill Inn although sometimes to the George. The Rail Mill was where the union meetings were held as well.

I got back on the staff and became a shift clerk at the 12in mill and about two years after that I was made a shift foreman. Then I found my experience on the shop floor really useful. At Parkgate generally it was very rare for someone on the shop floor to be promoted on to the staff. Later I became a dispatch foreman, then a senior clerk and then a section manager on the 10in mill (which closed in 1969). In 1965 I was involved with training schemes for operatives at Parkgate and Tommy Booth, who had been one of the rollers, was involved in that.

Gordon Read

Crossland's Foundry

My father started at the Crossland's Foundry back in the 1920s. He said that the foundry had been Turkish Baths before he took it over. His mother's maiden name was Care and she had first come over to England following the Potato Famine. He persuaded his cousin, Edmund Crossland, to join the firm. Edmund was a moulder at Yates and Hayward's at the time. The foundry used to be made up of the fettling shop, the casting shop and the canteen. The offices were upstairs. It was re-modelled in the 1950s and all made open plan with the machine shop at one end. The wooden patterns for light castings were hung up on the balcony that surrounded the machine shop. There were castings for petrol pumps and drain grates amongst many other things.

When I was young my dad used to take me down to the foundry on Saturday morning so he could grind the rough edges off the castings. He used to wear a leather apron when he used the grinding wheel. I was allowed to play in the sand that was always around in the works because of the casting. He used to finish at dinner time and then we would call at Schonhut's on the way home. We used to get pork pies, sausage rolls and even bread from Schonhut's. It was always a very clean shop even at the back and Leonard Schonhut was a big friend of my dad. The Schonhuts used to live in a house attached to the shop; I can remember it was all done with wooden panelling and there was a grand piano in the front room.

Helena Ward

A rare view of the inside of Crossland's Foundry in Parkgate.

Some of the workforce at Crossland's Foundry in Foundry Street.

Pit or steelworks

At Haugh Road School I was in the A form, the top form, all the way through and always in the top ten in the class. When I was leaving school I was sent down to the Methodist chapel in Rawmarsh High Street to talk to a careers officer. Basically he said to me what do you want, pit or steelworks? That was the only choice you got. I went to Aldwarke Colliery and worked there from being fifteen in 1953 till it closed in 1961. Aldwarke was almost like a family pit. It was a very hot pit; it was just like you were working under a shower. You had to have a saline drink when you came out of the pit. It was so hot because you were working far out away from the shaft. I started with a ten-week course at Manvers and then I went straight down the pit. I was involved in haulage at first. They still had four horses down the pit there then. Most pits had got rid of all their horses by then. There was a big horse there called Peter and they used to use him on the pit bottom. I wanted to be in the money so as soon as I was eighteen I asked to go on the coal face. I should have been supervised for the first three weeks but on my second day he was off and I was left on my own. There was an accident near me when an old miner about sixty years old got his leg caught under a tub. I had to stop the rope and go and see to him. I did what I could till somebody came.

We used a longwall system, undercutting the coal and then blasting. Then you had a stint (or pog) of coal that was 11 yards. It was a twenty-four-hour cycle with a 5ft advance before the coal was undercut and blasted again. You worked on your own. Where you were in teams was in the ripping. I started in the Parkgate seam that was 4ft 6in to 5ft high, but the Silkstone seam was only 2ft high so you had to lie down to work it. The Silkstone seam always paid better than the Parkgate seam. Although it was low in the Silkstone the conditions were good, but in the Parkgate the rocks above were called clod and kennel and they kept collapsing without warning. The kennel was really sharp and it could cut you badly if it fell on you. All the coal in the Parkgate seam was hand-got.

There were about 400 miners at Aldwarke when it closed. They reckoned it was closed down because they wanted to build the new steel mill at Thybergh. I moved over to Kilnhurst pit from Aldwarke.

Danny Larder

Office boy at Parkgate steelworks

I started as an office boy at Parkgate steelworks in the late 1950s. It was the duty of the office boy each morning to go round the office and take orders for the shops in Broad Street – so many Woodbines, so many Players Navy Cut, some sandwiches from Staniforth and so on. You used to take a cardboard box and all the orders. Each office at Parkgate seemed to have a particular shop in Parkgate to get most of the stuff from. One morning as I was taking the order into Parkgate my aunt, Ruth Purdy (she later married Leonard Schonhut), who worked in Schonhut's beckoned me over and said, 'Why don't you buy all your stuff from our shop?' I asked how I could get cigarettes from there, but she said

Malcolm and Noreen Brown in Skegness in 1959. It was about this time Malcolm started working at the steelworks.

she would get them from Bailey's to sell in Schonhut's. So for two or three days I shopped at Schonhut's. Then it got back to the original shop what I was doing and there was an enquiry at work and I had to stop. There might have been up to twenty lads shopping in Parkgate for different offices in the works and then they were coming off the shop floor

A stunning window display in Schonhut's shop, where Malcolm made some unusual orders.

as well. The shops in Parkgate used to be little gold mines with all those workers at the steelworks going in and out every day. For the first half of the twentieth century not much really changed in the works and the way it operated. Once the works moved its site to Aldwarke and Roundwood in the 1960s things began to change and far less of the workers regularly went into Broad Street and Rawmarsh Hill.

Malcolm Brown

Boxing Day start

I started at New Stubbin on Boxing Day 1954, just before my fifteenth birthday. I went to Manvers first for training and then started on haulage down the pit. I was in haulage in the Parkgate seam first and then moved on to the Silverwood seam. I started my coalface training when I was twenty-one and went on the Low End at the north-east; that was

Ray Hague who went into mining just before his fifteenth birthday.

about 4-4½ft high. I worked at New Stubbin until 1977 and I thought it was a good pit. Then they asked for volunteers to go to Cortonwood and as we knew Stubbin was winding down I went there and worked till 1985 when they shut it down after many bitter battles. Then I went to Treeton until that closed in 1988. I've been out of work ever since apart from two years in the gardens at the Earth Centre.

Ray Hague

Fined for taking bets

I grew up on Netherfield Lane and the house is still there. When I was there there was no electricity and no bathroom. My father was James Concannon and he came to Aldwarke Road, Parkgate, with his family from Galway in Ireland. My mother was from Rotherham and came to live in Parkgate. My dad was a bookie and drove an ambulance and my mum delivered milk for the Co-op. It was illegal to be a bookie then and people came to place bets in my grandma's parlour. You were only allowed to bet on the horses if you went to the race track. Every now and then my dad would be fined by the police for taking illegal bets and had to pay about 2s 6d. The policeman who fined him might have been there an hour before placing a bet! He was probably fined about every eight or ten weeks. He used to have these cast-iron boxes to put the bets in which showed the time when they were closed.

Yvonne Harrison

six

PEOPLE AND PLACES

Memories of High Street

As I remember it, when I was young High Street was quite picturesque, with many old cottages and gardens. The Star Inn was built of stone and faced down to Parkgate. It had quaint windows, as did the Earl Grey, which fronted directly onto the narrow pavement. Pottery Street, next to the Earl Grey, went from the High Street, but with no width for vehicles really. A large council yard took up quite a large area next to the inn. Adjoining that, there were some tiny cottages and shops. One was a cobbler's owned by Cronjie, and there was Steel's confectioners, a barber's shop and a pawn shop belonging to Stella Ashton's father. Nearby was Milnes' shop, or shops, as one sold furniture and the other footwear. Behind was a very large yard called Providence Place with five cottages. Harold Allen lived in one of the cottages.

Across from the cottages were two garages, a stable and a wash kitchen. Above the stable was a large room with a wooden floor and a fireplace. Apparently this was used as a meeting room before the chapel was built across the road. Mr Milnes used to have a horse and dray to take out the furniture to customers. A very high wall was found at the bottom of the yard and we used to climb it when the fair came with its roundabouts and stalls. Across the road was the Manor House owned by the artist George Burden and his wife. They were big friends of ours and we played there a lot as there were farm buildings at the back. The large barn contained a tractor and other vehicles that went with it. When the traction engine driver drove out early in the morning I thought he would crash into our house as there was so little space to turn round.

Mollie Cooper

Mollie Cooper (*née* Milnes) is shown here on the left with her mother Blanche and her sister Christine. They were on a visit to Filey.

Living on Green Lane

I was born at 40 Green Lane, the farm was still there in the lane at that time, but it was knocked down more than fifty years ago. It was lovely in Green Lane then. Green Lane Tavern was on the corner of Greenfield Lane (later to be Barber's Avenue). On the other corner was a general shop called Hague's; it sold groceries and sweets. A bit further up there was a big grocer's shop called Tiptaft's next to the Crown Inn and on the opposite side to where we lived.

My parents were Herbert Simpson and Annie, whose family name was Painter before she married. Dad was a rope splicer at Warren House Colliery, his family lived in Parkgate. We lived in one of the top three houses in Green Lane and they were joined up to three cottages. At the back they looked onto Chapel Street and New Street. The Goss family lived next door one way and the Marcroft family was on the other side. Eva Marcroft was a friend of mine, along with my cousin Elsie Painter. When they decided the cottages had to be demolished they said our houses would have to come down as well. We had to move up to Monkwood then. We used Scales as a butcher's and we lived just below the fish and chip shop; my mother said the Steels originally ran it, but I remember when it was the Souths. There was a gents' hairdresser near the Crown.

Edith Schofield

People of Pottery Street

I was born at 78 Pottery Street, the thirteenth house down. The top half of the street were older houses than the bottom, but they all looked the same really. There was a space left for gardens at the top, but they were not used for that, so the kids used to play there; it was called the Croft. The street was nearly all arranged in six houses to a yard. My grandfather lived in the top house and that was much bigger. They had a big living place [room], a big room at the side and a big kitchen. They had three bedrooms upstairs as well. My mum and dad lived there at first when they were married and my big sister was born there.

Most of the men in the street were miners rather than steelworkers. Alick Jeffery's family lived at Number 92; his father was a miner and called Alick as well. His Uncle Horace lived next door. There was a bookies in the street and of course gambling was illegal then. The bookie was Horace Murfin and he lived on the other side of the street to us. The police were always trying to catch people gambling, but there were men on lookout to give warnings. One day Reggie Ellis's milk wagon, filled with hay, came up the street and stopped and from below the hay a lot of bobbies jumped out and rushed into the bookie's house. My dad, Ernest Evans [Kufftee], was on the table pretending to change a light bulb, but as he only had one arm it wasn't a very good excuse!

Betty Watts

Chapel Street, the oldest of the long terraced streets in Rawmarsh. Many of the residents here would have been regulars at the Kilnhurst Co-op.

The Kilnhurst Races

At the Co-op you could have 'tick' on a quarterly basis, but on what was called Quarter Monday everything had to be paid up. On Tuesday we had stock-taking and then on the Wednesday you could have as much 'tick' as you wanted and for the next three months, although the boss had to approve every request for 'tick'. It was the son of Councillor Hutchinson who became manager of the Kilnhurst Co-op. The nickname for the Quarter Mondays was the Kilnhurst Races because so many people came on those days. I think they even ran special trains from Rotherham for all the people paying up for their three months of credit. The easiest way for people from Rotherham to get to Kilnhurst was by train. Eventually they started running a bus from Ainleys, at the crossroads in Parkgate, to Kilnhurst. That was just before the war. All the members used to have a cheque card and at the Kilnhurst Co-op we paid the best 'divvy' in the whole area, 3s in the pound. They only got 2s in the pound in Rotherham.

Muriel Sykes

On Aldwarke Road

Nearby were the white toll gates where a woman came out of a little house to collect money from any vehicles. The road was quite busy because there was Aldwarke Main Colliery as well as two railway stations and two big stone houses where two of the bosses from Parkgate Iron and Steel Works lived. The houses were called Granby House and Linton House. Close to our house was Christ Church and the school beside it. Mr Thirkell taught my brother in the Sunday school there.

Just the other way was a big house where the Misses Tiptaft lived. They had their own tennis court. We thought that was marvellous! Later the house became the Aldwarke Road Working Men's Club. Dr Naylor had a surgery close by too. Beyond that there were the meadows that often flooded and in icy weather between the wars people went skating there. We went down to watch them skate and there would be people selling hot roast chestnuts. A bit nearer home, on the other side of the road, was Station Row and close by an area we played in that we called the Daisy Field.

We had a passage below our house and beyond that Mr Lee had a shop that sold household crockery and cooking pans. Mr Lee had a son called Frank Carnelly Lee and he set up a choir at New Stubbin Colliery that was quite famous. He also had snap tins and water bottles for the colliers. The colliers used to bring their pick axes to him for sharpening. In my memory I can hear the colliers going to work with their heavy boots or clogs and their snap tins. Their bottles used to rattle as they hung from their belts.

Nellie Schofield

One of the big houses on Aldwarke Road where Nellie Schofield remembers a boss at the steelworks lived.

A rare view of the floods affecting the Meadows. Aldwarke Colliery can be seen in the background.

The High Street close to Moxon's Yard. Notice all the steam from Whitlam's fish and chip shop.

Moxon's Yard

There was a house in Moxon's Yard where the Strattons lived. You stepped straight into their main room because it was a shop as well. They had a dresser on one side and there would be sweets in jars displayed there. They also sold Seidlitz Powder for biliousness. The table was in the middle of the room and they, mum, dad and Ada the daughter, might be sat on big high-backed chairs there having dinner when you went in to buy something. There would be a big coal fire blazing and they were always open.

The shop at the top of Moxon's Yard was the Misses Fowlers' and they were hairdressers. I went there for my first perm when it was first wired up for electricity. There was 'Cronjie' Marsh, who was a cobbler, nearby. Then there was Holroyd's shop. Mrs Holroyd lived in a house near Clark's business. It had windows down the side and she used to sell wools and things for embroidery. Her shop window was always well set out. There was Womack's fish and chip shop and Cartwright's toy shop.

Marjorie Oxer

Lloyd Street Primitive Methodist (Bethel)

My parents were married at Bethel Chapel in 1926 and my brother and I were baptised there. It was a typical Victorian building – ancillary rooms downstairs, extensive hall and worship area with balcony on the first floor. Services and meetings included worship and Sunday school twice each Sunday, Christian Endeavour, Sisterhood, Choir practice, Men's meeting, concerts, plays and Whitsuntide celebrations. I well remember being sent home from Sunday school on 3 September 1939 to await Neville Chamberlain's announcement that the country was at war.

The time came to seriously consider the future of the premises and the decision was taken to unite with the St Paul's Wesleyan Church on Broad Street and become Parkgate Methodist Church. At this time the steel industry was expanding and many people turned out to witness the arrival of two fearsome-looking blast furnaces on the back of two lengthy transporters. The land on which Bethel stood was owned by the steel company and the premises were eventually turned into a canteen for the use of the work force. Sadly, it was gutted by fire in 1961 and the site was razed to the ground.

Marian Overland

Dad was in the band

Dad played the trombone in the Rawmarsh Prize Band and he used to practise at home. He played in the band from the age of fourteen. It was lovely music; no one ever used to

A view of High Street, including the Star public house. The Prize Band practised close to the Star.

complain. They were a very good band. They went down to London to play at the Crystal Palace. 1921 was a really good year for them; they won all the competitions they went in for. The band used to play in Rosehill Park quite often, on the bandstand. Lots of people listened to them there. They also gave concerts in Clifton Park. I used to take round the collecting tin at the concerts. They used to practise in the Band Room, which was a place across the yard from the Star. People used to go there to listen to them practise. The band usually led the parade through Rawmarsh at Whitsuntide.

Edith Schofield

Raised on the Monkey Island

I was born and brought up on Infirmary Road with my six sisters. That part of Parkgate was always referred to as the 'Island' or even the 'Monkey Island'. There were two rows of houses stretching down to the Victoria Mission (where Mr McCloskey was the preacher) and the waste ground next to it was called the 'Hollow' where we played football. There always seemed to be a lot of activity in the Hollow off Infirmary Road. Sometimes there would be a 'tingle-airy' man playing music with his performing monkey and begging for money and at other times there would by people flying their Japanese kites. You could buy the kites for threepence or sixpence.

There were six houses in our row, but none of the roads were properly surfaced there. The four houses at the end of Infirmary Road and Victoria Road were called Thrybergh View. There were no pavements all the way along to the new road [Barber's Avenue]. Behind the tin hut of the mission there was a fantastic football pitch and a really good team called Christ Church played there. They were nearly on a level with Rotherham United, but that would have been before I was born. There was a pavilion there called the 'stripping hut' to get changed in. Sammy Chapman played there and he went to play for Rotherham. Sam Hassell was a goalkeeper who played for Parkgate Welfare and I used to stand behind his goal and watch his moves.

There was a brick building on Infirmary Road that had been an infirmary once and when I was a kid over the building there were the letters I O G T (or I Owe Gertie Tuppence as we used to call it). It was a religious building and they used to have uniforms on that had embroidered jackets and collars. I think the letters stood for the Independent Order of Good Templars. One day when the weather was bad and there was nowhere to play we broke in and found the room filled with benches. This must have been around 1935. Later it was turned into a scissors factory.

Cliff Hawley

Living on Pottery Street

Butcher Gascoigne was a boxer and he lived up our street and so did Rag Elsie. She used to collect rags for sale. She looked like Hannah Hauxwell. Fat Jack used to hang around with her. Elsie would let you have a blow down her trumpet if you gave her some rags. Elsie lived opposite us. The Prices lived up the street from us and they used to keep a pig in the kitchen under the table! My grandad lived in the top house and that was next to the open space that was the drying ground for the houses at the top of the street. That was where we played football, cricket and had our bonfire. My grandad's house wall had football posts and cricket stumps drawn on it.

One old fella, Sammy Cartwright, had a grocery shop in his front room in Pottery Street. He lived opposite the Prices and their pig. There were also two little sweet shops in the street; there was Mrs Hawke's, and the Dudhills had one on our side of the street. We also went to Foxton's bakery that was down to the bottom of the street and just round the corner. At the bottom of Chapel Street was Stan Robinson and he was a crippled cobbler. Near there was a chip shop in Green Lane and you had to go up some steps to get into it. At that time people used to come round selling blocks of salt door-to-door. There was also a Jewish man who came round on a bike with glass on his back. He used to mend windows, but if people wouldn't pay once he had put in a new pane he had a hammer to break it!

Albert Evans

Trading on Green Lane

Tiptaft's shop was at the top of Green Lane. It was next to the old Crown pub. It was a grocer's shop, but I think it had changed hands before the war started. The cycle shop on Green Lane was Cotterill's. The Burdens had a farm on Green Lane; I went to school with their Kathleen. It was still operating as a farm when I was going to school; I remember them selling milk. During the war my mother used to let the milk stand and then skim off the cream to try and make butter.

Marjorie Oxer

Tiptaft's shop at the top of Green Lane is still remembered by some today, even though it has been closed for over fifty years.

The community of Wheatcroft Road

We moved to Wheatcroft Road from New Street in 1938. My brother Geoff was born a few weeks after we moved. My dad was a miner at New Stubbin pit. It was a bit traumatic at first because the pit went on to short time. I think they used to sound a siren if there was no work, so if you heard the siren you stayed at home and got no pay of course. Once the war came it all changed – it was all hands to the pumps. I think we paid about £300 for the house, which was a lot of money then. Dad carried on in the pit until he retired. One side of Wheatcroft Road was all old terraced houses and on the other side they built new houses. We all moved in within a few weeks of each other. We had electric lights instead of gas lights, but we only had one plug in the living room. That was all right when mum used a flat iron but when she moved on to an electric iron, I wanted her to speed up so I could listen to the radio. Because dad was a miner we had plenty of coal, so we had fires in both rooms. The kitchen was tiny and at the side of the house. All the cooking was done on the open coal fire – the range.

There were children in every house so it was a real good community. We knew the names of just about everybody up and down the street. After the war they brought people in from Ireland to tarmac the road and we all had to take them in as lodgers. The lodger we had was a big man and very quiet. I think he stopped for a few months. He had his meals with us at home.

Joyce Bray

A view of Wheatcroft Road with its unmade road surface.

The full cast of *Country Girl* performed by the Parkgate Operatic Society.

A newspaper advertisement for the 1944 production of *The Gondoliers*.

Four of the
principals from
the performance
of *The Gondoliers*
including Brenda
Birks, Joan
Mitchell and Jack
Grayson.

Singing with the Parkgate Operatic Society

I have always loved singing and when I was young I sang with the Parkgate Operatic
Society. Most of the people in the society then were from Parkgate. The shows were
produced at the Miners' Institute at first, but later they moved to the Regent in Rotherham.
We practised in Ashwood Road School and put on shows like *The Arcadians*, *Tom Jones*,
Merrie England, *The Gondoliers* and *Rebel Maid*. Our productions were some of the main
features of the Rotherham Holidays-at-Home programme. Miss Pansy Moore was both
the producer and the director and a real tartar! The humorous parts were often taken by
Coltie Acom and Albert Hawke, but during the war there was a real shortage of men.
I used to go straight from work to the practices so I would leave home at eight in the
morning and not get back till eleven at night. Even during the war we were able to hire
the lovely dresses you can see in the photos.

Joan Gillions

Cattle on the road

Close to the Travellers pub there was a little cobbler's shop where people had their
shoes mended. I think the cobbler did a bit of book-making on the quiet! When I was
growing up there were four or five butchers' shops in Parkgate and some had their own

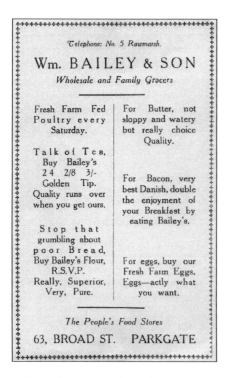

Left: An advertisement for Bailey's grocers shop, which Nellie Schofield remembers well and where Betty Watts started work. *Right*: Wannop's shop in Broad Street was around long enough to have a street named after it. This picture shows it trading under the name of Wannop & Foxton.

slaughterhouses. I recall cattle being driven down past our house to the slaughterhouses, having been unloaded at Aldwarke Road station. One of the butchers, Schonhut's, was attacked in the First World War because they were Germans. On Saturday afternoons you could take your basin to Schonhut's and get hot roast pork put in it. Mrs Schonhut always used to say 'Gravy? Stuffing?' They made their own black pudding and polony. Generally their shops were very popular and Bill's was good as well. We used to go to Wannop's sometimes for ham; they cut it in nice thick slices. It was a good shop was Wannop's. Bailey's was another grocer's in Parkgate and there was Lowe's gentlemen's outfitters next door. Smith's was a big shop too that sold everything in the clothing line. You could buy really good class shoes there. I remember Tommy Tildesley, the herbalist, as well. There were two pawnbrokers in Parkgate and they did a good trade.

Nellie Schofield

At 'Romish Feast'

We used to go to the fair in Rawmarsh on the fairground. The Feast then was at the beginning of August. The engines used to come up Dale Road, *Majestic* and *Thunderer* pulled the wagons with the rides on. The fairground was at the top of Green Lane. Some of the big rides were Noah's Ark, Sky Rocket and Swish. There were 'chairoplanes' as well. A lot of the stalls were 'penny roll-downs'. We used to crawl right under all the rides and play 'iddy' [hide and seek] with all the machinery spinning around above us – no health and safety in those days!

There was always a boxing booth; if you could last three rounds you won 10*s*. Most of them that tried to win on Bosco's Boxing Booth were men coming home from the pub at night. Some of the miners like the Briggs and the Rooks kidded 'Champ' Hague to go in the ring and he stripped to the waist with his braces on and his Oxford bags. He'd been drinking and he got seven bells knocked out of him. He went wading in swinging his arms around, and he was a big lad, but it was no good, his face ended up like a squashed tomato. He got killed at New Stubbin pit later. They reckon it was all a bit of a cheat because the challengers were always given big soft gloves, but the booth boxer had proper boxing

Some of the lads from Romish Feast, including; Maurice Hawley, Ron Liversidge, John Lewis and John Turner. They are shown here on a camping trip in the Hope Valley, *c.* 1948.

gloves that were a bit harder. Some of the older lads used to do a bit of boxing in our yard in New Street. I can remember my brother, Bob Seekings, Terry Machin and the Scholeys having a go. In all the Romish Feast used to last about a week. It wasn't just a great event for kids – even our grandparents got excited when the fair arrived. Eventually it moved to Rosehill Park.

Ron Liversidge

'The Mail' trolleybus

There used to be a trolleybus came up from Swinton, through Rawmarsh and on to Rotherham and it was called 'The Mail'. Rotherham was written in red on the front of the bus and inside there was a box where you posted your letters. You could stop it anywhere and use it and any mail posted there would be delivered next morning to any address in Rotherham. It started off from Brook Square, Conisbrough at eight o'clock at night and got to the Woodman at half-past eight. As a child you had to be in the house around the time of The Mail so you could run up the road with any letters from your parents. It ran right up to the beginning of the Second World War.

Harold Badger

A line of trolleybuses standing on the road near the tram sheds.

Ryecroft life

We used to hear the miners walking to Kilnhurst pit every day with their clogs on. They always had their 'dudleys' with them with water in. We used to take our accumulator down Main Street to Sam Turner's newsagents shop. There were two cobblers locally; one was Horace Pursglove, who had a shop like a wooden shed past Sandhill Road. He lost a leg in the First World War. Then there was Benny Carr, whose shop was opposite Main Street where the tracklesses turned. He was deaf and dumb, so he used to write the price of the repair on the sole of the shoe with the day to be collected.

One of the local characters was Vic Bullens, who was a bookmaker. He used to stand near the telephone box at the top of South Street. When the police came he used to run down South Street and down the passage next to our house and over the wall. There also used to be a man in the 1940s who pushed a pram round full of pieces of sandstone to use for cleaning the back window sill and the back door step. A small piece was a penny and a big piece for tuppence. He used to get them from the cemetery when they dug a new grave. You also did the whole of your front step and the whole of your front window sill because no one ever came in that way apart from the doctor.

Tommy Longden used to go round on his bike lighting all the gas lamps. He got so good he didn't even need to get off his bike to light them. He worked for the council and drove the steam roller. We had no electricity in our house until the late 1940s.

Crawshaw's greengrocers was at the top of South Street, we got our fruit and vegetables there; they used to sell 'specked fruit' cheap. They also used to skin rabbits in the shop. Frank's grandfather always said that the Crawshaws had started their shops because they were supposed to have black-legged in the General Strike; they used to work in Kilnhurst Colliery. When they went back to the colliery at the end of the strike no one would work with them, so they used the money to get the shops. Downs' sweet shop was at the park end of the road and towards the end of the war they got iced lollipops. They used to turn puréed apple into lollies.

Frank Horner and Margaret Pursglove before their marriage.

Margaret Horner

Doctors on call

At that time before the war there were several doctors in Rawmarsh; there was Dr O'Connell, Dr Lister, Dr Jockill on Westfield Road, and, a bit later, Dr Coppin, who was on Dale Road. There was a Dr Philpott working with Dr O'Connell and he lived in the old detached house in Kilnhurst Road. Gambling always went on even though it was illegal. One of the bookies in Rawmarsh used to sit on a seat beside the Horse and Jockey and do his business from there. My mother used to tell me that they would all run away if the police came. She also told me of the knocker-up going round to wake all the miners in the morning and about the night-soil men who came to clear out the toilets and the middens. One of the local shops I can remember was Ena and Phil Gooch's sweet shop on Stocks Lane. We used to go there during the war. There was a flower shop below that and then Spick's Yard. The Co-op nearby had a system of wires running across the shop to carry bills and money to the cashier and then back.

Sheila Skeldon

The end of the chapel on Hollybush

There was a big Methodist chapel across the road from us at the end of Hollybush. It was the headquarters for the local Home Guard during the war. It was knocked down not long after the war. I can remember the first thing the steeplejack did was to dismantle the top part of the spire and lower it down to the ground. It was knocked down from the top

downwards. One gable end had a rope put round it and then it was hooked up to a lorry on Hollybush Street and pulled down. When it was all pulled down that used to be our playground. It was left derelict for years. Bob Davis came shortly after the war and bought the first shop up the hill. He was a barber. Then he started a taxi business and built a garage there.

Danny Larder

Danny Larder lived on Hollybush Street. Pictured here are his mother, father and grandma outside the house.

Gambling games

Everyone was a miner down New Street then. On some Sunday afternoons I can remember they used to come back from the pub and have running races in the street and they used to bet on the results. They were stripped off to the waist and ran from the top to the bottom of New Street. Gambling was still illegal then. The two street bookmakers in New Street were Herbie Billups and Bob Carr. There were a lot of bets placed on something like the Grand National, but usually only about 3*d* each way. One day the police raided the street to catch people gambling. Herbie Billups ran into my dad's house and hid under the table.

There was a tossing ring in Brigg's Yard at Johnny 'Cobbler' Lewis's. If the police came everyone ran off. There were two exits: one by Silverwood's shop next to the 'Palady' and one down the snicket to Chapel Street. The big building in New Street we called the 'Palady' which was our name for the Palais de Dance. There was boxing and wrestling there at one time and an ice rink. At the top of New Street across the road there was Walker Scales' butchers shop, Copes' sweet shop, Nelson's cobblers, Maurice Hawley's and Fisher's beer-off. There was the Horse and Jockey as well. The Primitive Methodist Chapel I can remember. It had a big balcony in it. At one time after the war it was filled with monkey-nuts [groundnuts] after some scheme or other. It was linked up with Strachey, the Food Minister. They were going to turn them into margarine. Eventually some lorries came to collect them, but some kids split the bags so there were plenty lying around on the ground!

Ron Liversidge

Walker Scales standing by the Yorkshire range behind his butcher's shop in Dale Road. He worked there until well into his nineties.

The Scales family. Walker's father had run the butcher's shop for years before Walker took over.

The Crossland family enjoying a day out at Roche Abbey. Father O'Riordan had words to say to them.

St Joseph's Church

The school was built first, as was usual then in new Catholic parishes. The Masses were said in the school. They could pull back the partitions between the three rooms to make more room for Mass. At one time the parish tried to buy the old chapel in Dale Road to use as a Catholic church, but it fell through. There was a flourishing dramatic society at St Joseph's at one time and when the church was finally built in Green Lane its design was based on the idea of using it for theatrical performances as well as for church services, but after it was finished it was decided that there should not be any plays put on there. When the services were in the school there were two Masses on Sunday, one at 8.30 a.m. and one at 10.30 a.m. We had a really fiery priest at that time called Father O'Riordan. I was a Crossland before I got married and the priest used to say 'If you see the Sheerans on the way to Mass you are late and if you see the Crosslands you are very late!' Bryan and I were one of the first couples to get married in the church.

Helena Ward

Rawmarsh Cricket Club

Most weekends we spent at the cricket club at Barber's Avenue. It was only a wooden-hut affair with a billiard table in the middle and two small rooms, but everyone was friendly and knew one another. They had some wise old birds at Rawmarsh CC; they bought the land (about 8.9 acres) in 1926 for around £1,800 and sold a strip to the council for the same price to make what is now Barber's Avenue. Owning your own club was a big thing

Some of Jim Evans' 'wise old birds' at the Cricket Club in Rawmarsh. Jim himself is furthest right on the front row.

because most clubs in the area were brewery subsidised. There were two cricket teams, one in the Yorkshire League and one in the Doncaster League. Both teams fielded some very good local talent like Bottomley, who went on to play with Yorkshire. My brother Jack was steward there during the war period and then his daughter Phyllis and her husband Jack Whitworth took over. The Whitworths, Ernest and Jack, were always cricket-mad and would always give a hand to keep things running.

By now they were engaging artists at the weekend with our Gertie on piano. There were no mics at this time so the acts had to be able to sing. Doreen Beals from Leeds was a great soprano and even Tony Daly sang there for £5 and he became one of the finest tenors going. Things were going well and in 1958 the old wooden hut gave way to a new £12,000 Concert Room with an organ.

The competition between clubs was getting greater and artistes from all over were being introduced through agents to the big club at Greasbrough run by Les Booth. To keep in the running we had an even bigger Concert Room built at a cost of £35,000 and opened up every night.

Jim Evans

Fishing on Greasbrough dams

I used to go fishing when I was young. I went up to Greasbrough dams or to the stream from the dam on the lowlands. I didn't pay anything then to fish. I just used a garden cane, a bit of string, a bent pin and a worm from the garden. I caught the usual fish: roach, perch and gudgeon. When I started at the pit it used to cost half a crown for a licence to fish in the dams. You could buy it at the pit. By then I had the proper tackle. When I came off night shift on a Saturday morning at about six o' clock I used to go fishing straight away. I took my rod, reel and keep-net to work and collected them at the end of the shift. I used to go down with two or three pals. When I got married Lesley used to come down in the afternoon with a flask and a couple of sandwiches. We used to spend hours down there. Later the permit went up to 7*s* 6*d*.

Ray Hague

Settling in at Low End

I was seven years old when I first came to live in Parkgate, in Stanley Street. I particularly remember the Creamer family, Alfred White, Frank Spencer (who lost his foot after he started work at Parkgate Iron and Steel Works), Joan Neatby, the Concannons and the Brothertons. I remember two local shops, one a grocery (Bonson's) and a beer-off (Brotherton's). Then there was Tolley's the newsagent and two local pubs, the Rail Mill and the one at the top of Stanley Street, the Rockingham, which was run by the Pardy family. The Flying Dutchman was further along under the bridge towards Stone Row. There was a lorry driven by Mr Staves that came down the street once or twice a week selling fruit and vegetables. There was also a little 'house shop' run by the Jefferies at the bottom of Stanley Street on the left-hand side where you could go and get oddments and it really was 'open all hours'. There was always a bookie called Toddy Price, or one of his runners,

standing at the top of the street or in the area. Folk would sidle up to him and slip him a bit of paper along with the money to place bets on the horses. There was always someone keeping an eye out for the police.

Les Coe

The Little Bridge Inn was close to Low End with several other pubs like the Flying Dutchman and the George.

The 'business end' of Schonhut's butchers. Not a favourite spot for Yvonne Harrison.

Broad Street, with its numerous shops that Yvonne Harrison remembers well.

Shops galore

After the war, I can remember going to Mrs Gregg's shop on the corner of Goosebutt Street for our butter and our sugar. It wasn't all packed up then; it had to be weighed up. That was instead of going all the way down to Bailey's. We used to go in Speight's as well for tripe, it was lovely. They were famous as well because they made all the pies. We used to go in on Saturday morning on the way to my nan's and we would take a jar to get our sloppy peas and another jar for the gravy. My dad was a friend of Leonard Schonhut and sometimes we used to go in the back of the shop, but I didn't like it because they were making things like black pudding with all the blood. Steel's bakery was down there as well. Smith's was at the bottom of Rawmarsh Hill and was a big haberdashery shop; it sold all sorts of materials. Near there, but on the Library side of the road, was Dixon's and that was a china shop. Lorraine and I used to go there to put our pocket money down for Christmas presents for our mum. Mum used to belong to a Savings Club there. Lower down there was a small Denham's shop as well. Parkgate was a lovely shopping centre.

Yvonne Harrison

The new television

In the year of the Queen's coronation I persuaded my dad to buy a television. There were only about three in the street. I told my dad that if he got a television he would be able to watch the Cup Final. I think that swung it! We watched the coronation at home with a crowd of other people. We were meant to go to Rosehill Park for a big celebration in the evening, but the rain was so bad it was called off. There was no street party because of the weather. The picture on the screen was really small and sometimes the programme did not come on when it was meant to. It wasn't really a rival to the cinema then because there weren't many programmes on the television. People used to listen to the radio a lot.

Joyce Bray

Living on Holm Flatt Street

Holm Flatt Street around 1960 had quite a lot of families from different parts of the world. There were several Irish families like us and down the street there were the Palmowski's, who originated from Poland. We went to school with them because they were Catholics like us and went to St Joseph's on Green Lane. Then there was a big Russian man who used to terrify us with his shouting when he was drunk. He had massive curls like Beethoven. He was a chef so he kept funny hours. Later I thought about the terrible things he might have seen in Russia before he came over. Occasionally there were Italian people around and a man that we thought was an Arab man, but thinking back now he might have been from Pakistan.

At times it was overcast with clouds of muck and smoke from the steelworks and the 'Chemics' but people used to say 'Breathe that in, it's good for you.' Further up the street there was one posh house and that belonged to Charlie Hague who owned the pop factory across the road. It was posh because it was bigger and had a garden with trees around it. He owned most of the houses at the top end of the street so people who worked for him had the houses.

I always remember the old men in the street who seemed very old and were worn out with work. There was Bill Cooper next door who walked very slowly and had a bad

One of the 'built-up' stretches of the stream close to Holm Flatt Street where Ray Hearne went exploring.

chest because he'd worked in the pit. Down the street was 'old man' Lockwood, who always seemed to be wheezing and gasping for breath because his lungs were choked with coal dust or something. He always wore an old hat with a brim. I remember the older women on the street always wore pinnies; they were bigger than aprons and wound round them. Lots of women went off to work and my mother at one time used to get collected by coach in Parkgate to go off to work at Batchelor's Peas. They all wore turbans on their hair to keep it tidy.

Ray Hearne

Storm of '62

In 1962 there was a terrible wind that damaged a lot of the houses in Parkgate and Rawmarsh. Jockey Gee was on the council then and all the building companies working for the council were called in to help with repairs. It took months to get them all sorted. There was a lot of damage around Netherfield Lane and it was filthy because a lot of ceilings had collapsed and years of dirt from Parkgate Forge came down with the ceilings. Our house in South Street got showered with tiles coming off the Co-op shop behind during the storm. Jockey Gee had a barrow and he used to advertise 'distance no object'. One story was that he once took a three-piece suite to Tickhill! He was quite a character; rates were going to be 6*d* in the pound when he got elected.

Freda Stacey

Other local titles published by The History Press

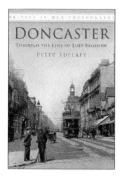

Doncaster: Through the Lens of Luke Bagshaw
PETER TUFFREY

This beautiful collection of photographs, taken from the original glass-plate negatives, showcases some of the very best of local photographer Luke Bagshaw's images of Doncaster in the late-nineteenth and early twentieth centuries. Each one of these photographs is extremely rare, including shots of the Great Northern Railway Co.'s engineering works. Every picture is accompanied by a detailed caption.

978 0 7524 4807 7

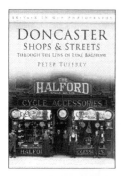

Doncaster Shops & Streets: Through the Lens of Luke Bagshaw
PETER TUFFREY

These nostalgic images capture the bygone days when independent retailers, such as Balby Laundry, E.H. Booth's grocers and Bell Brother's jewellers dominated the market place, as well as recording some of the earliest incarnations of well-known high street chains such as Boots and Halfords. With more than 200 images of stores and street scenes of yesteryear, this book captures a forgotten Doncaster.

978 0 7524 4837 4

Olde Yorkshire Punishments
HOWARD PEACH

This volume explores the darkest aspects of crime and punishment in Yorkshire over the centuries. From the stocks, joug and branding iron to the prison cell, galley – and noose – every punishment that could befall the criminals of Yorkshire is included in this volume. With sections on Church scandals, why bull-baiting was a legal requirement and the use of the Sharp Maiden – the guillotine – it will delight anyone with an interest in Yorkshire's history.

978 0 7524 4661 5

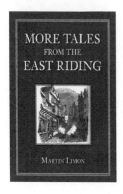

More Tales of the East Riding
MARTIN LIMON

Yorkshire's old East Riding has had a rich and varied past, and Martin Limon's second collection of historical stories is filled with more of the remarkable people, places and events that have made it that way. This volume contains stories of the East Riding's most famous residents, including William Wilberforce and Amy Johnson, alongside some forgotten aspects of the region's past – including the crime that shocked eighteenth-century Long Riston and health care in the area before the arrival of the NHS.

978 0 7524 4753 7

If you are interested in purchasing other books published by The History Press, or in case you have difficulty finding any History Press books in your local bookshop, you can also place orders directly through our website
www.thehistorypress.co.uk

Printed in Great Britain
by Amazon